OCCULT
IN THE WEST

Michael Willia[m]

BOSSINEY BOOKS

*First published in 1979
by Bossiney Books
St Teath, Bodmin, Cornwall
Typeset and printed in Great Britain by
Penwell Ltd, Parkwood, Callington,
Cornwall*

ISBN 0 906456 15 0

Plate Acknowledgements

Front cover by Paul Broadhurst
Back cover by Ray Bishop
9,11 David Halfyard
1,20,33 John Chard
3,12 Paul Broadhurst
6,8,29,30 Bryan Russell
2,10,13 Acora and Madam Jeannette
4,5,7,14,15,18,19,21-28 Ray Bishop
16,17 by courtesy of Jim Gregory
31,32,34,35 David Golby
36,37 Chris Chapman

About the Author

'Midsummer Eve 1965 was a memorable date for me,' recalls Michael Williams. 'A strange, inexplicable event, around midnight inside the Bossiney Methodist Chapel alongside Bossiney Mound changed my whole attitude to the Occult. From a few minutes after midnight I vowed never to adopt a cynical Doubting Thomas attitude about Supernatural possibility.'

In 1975 Michael Williams finished writing *Supernatural in Cornwall,* a factual approach to strange happenings in Cornwall defying logical explanation: a title that helped to firmly establish Bossiney Books as Cornish publishers. It is now in its fifth impression, and *Occult in the West* is its natural successor. 'In *Supernatural,* I restricted stories and interviews to Cornwall,' he explains, 'but in *Occult in the West,* I have cast a wider net, incorporating Devon as well. However, it's more than a longer journey in terms of sheer mileage. Psychic painting, auras, hypnosis and luck — these are only some of the Occult subjects I have explored for the first time. Hopefully, too, I have dug more deeply into aspects like clairvoyancy, healing and the psychic qualities of animals.'

With his wife Sonia, Michael Williams runs Bossiney Books from a cottage in North Cornwall — they are literally Cornish cottage publishers concentrating on Westcountry subjects.

For ten years they ran the Bossiney House Hotel, just outside Tintagel — hence the name Bossiney Books. Then in 1975 they left the hotel business and moved to St Teath to take up full-time publishing. This is their fiftieth title.

Despite the rapid growth of Bossiney Books — over forty titles in three years — Michael Williams has managed to make time to continue his own writing. This is his eighth title and he is currently writing about Port Isaac and the surrounding countryside and coastline — 'one of the most underestimated and underwritten bits of Cornwall'.

OCCULT
IN THE WEST

'Michael,' said the tarot card reader, 'you're going to write a book about the Supernatural, and it's related to Cornwall.'

I had no reason to suppose she knew about my researches into this very subject, and her prediction had an even more eerie ring when a fortnight later I was looking at a small wooden box in Tintagel Church, containing her ashes. She had died in her sleep and now her words rang like a real omen.

By the end of the month, I started writing, attempting to turn notes into a book. *Supernatural in Cornwall* was the result, one of the titles that helped to establish Bossiney Books, and five years on, it's still selling. Yet I found it a difficult book to finish. During the course of writing it, I interviewed more than sixty people and bringing some of those interviews to a close had been more complex than politely halting the conversation, for a handshake and a good-bye at the door had not always been the end of the story.

Take, for example, Lucretia Kelly of Falmouth who, in *Supernatural in Cornwall,* had talked about her wartime boyfriend — how a certain Alan Clayton had apparently died with the sinking of *HMS Hunter* in a Norwegian fjord. But unusual circumstances came to light in researching and writing that story, so unusual that Mrs Kelly decided to do a little amateur detective work. Thanks to the help of an ex-Naval colleague, she discovered the man was still alive!

'It was a strange feeling after all these years — nearly forty — to learn that he was alive . . . I'd been given his address but I was undecided about writing after so many years. But then I thought ''Why not?'' So I wrote telling him about the wartime experience and had a letter back by return with newspaper cuttings and photographs. He told me about the sinking of *HMS Hunter* and about his being a prisoner-of-war for five years and one month.' So Lucretia's horrific vision of Alan as 'a skeleton' — Chapter 18 in *Supernatural in Cornwall* — had been accurate to a considerable degree. He had come close to death with the sinking of his ship; there were times during the war when he seemed destined to a living death; and he emerged from his prisoner-of-war experience almost a physical skeleton, measured against his previous physique and weight. Furthermore,though now married, the two families met and became good friends — an event resulting from the book. Indeed it was an odd experience to receive a telephone call from 'a dead man' one Sunday morning, thanking me for the fact that the book had brought it all about.

So, in a very real way, this book is the daughter of the first. 'Life goes on, one experience leading to another' had been prophetic words. There had been a visit to a frightened family living in a bungalow in St Buryan Parish, frightened on account of strange, inexplicable noises — a psychic bombardment? As I drove away, questions shaped themselves. What would you do in their shoes? Ask for a service of exorcism, in the hope of removing some evil spirit? Or seek the services of a psychic investigator preferably a Spiritualist? Or merely call the Police?

Not long after, the building went up in flames and the marriage broke up. In the light of that kind of experience, I am no cynic.

The author C. S. Lewis once said in his whole life he had only met one person who had claimed to have seen a ghost, and as the lady did not believe in an immortal soul, she persisted in her disbelief, insisting that it must have been an illusion — or that she had suffered from some trick of nerves. So clearly seeing is not always believing.

However, inside these pages are only accounts and opinions of people who have convinced me of their sincerity. From first interview to the last, facts have been the aim. Though, in some cases, the facts may read more strangely than some fiction.

Evidence, in most Occult matters, though, *is* a matter of seeing *and* believing. Certainly during this Devon and Cornwall tour of strange experiences, some most interesting strands of evidence came from Sonia Theobald. A nurse for more than twenty years, Sonia Theobald has seen more than her share of death. Tall, blonde and with eyes usually associated with psychic qualities, she is realistic on the subject of life and death. We talked in Cornwall, but her strange sighting had been at Newton Abbot more than twenty years ago, at the home of her mother, Helen Hannafore. 'My grandmother was aged 97. A remarkable woman, she'd never had a doctor or a dentist, but she was now failing, and my mother, my sister Peggy and I were sitting in a groundfloor room which had been turned into grandmother's bedroom. It was between 11 o'clock and midnight, there was a grate in the room and a fire going, and the door leading to the hall was open. Grandmother was sleeping peacefully, and I remarked how well she was looking all things considered.

'Suddenly all three of us had this vision! A little old lady, the size of grandmother, went by the door. At first, I thought, "Why, I'm seeing things, I must be more tired than I thought". . . admittedly I'd had a long day nursing at the hospital . . . and then suddenly it, she — it was grandmother in older form — appeared again. And all the while grandmother lay sleeping soundly in her bed!

'My mother said "Did you see that?" "Yes," said my sister. So all three of us saw this vision not once but twice, and at five o'clock that morning grandmother just slept away and out of this life. Those two visions, before midnight, had been almost a signal that she was about to depart this life.'

For all her experience and the day-to-day business of caring for the sick and the old, Sonia Theobald makes no bones about her belief in angels. In fact, I'm convinced that my grandmother *is* my guardian angel. I'm often very conscious of her presence, and the interesting thing is that a clairvoyant told me about her, described her physically and accurately and said the letter E was prominent . . . grandmother *was* Emma or perhaps I should say *is* Emma.'

So for those three women in Newton Abbot seeing was believing — a rare case of a shared sighting.

So on this second Supernatural journey, I have crossed the Tamar, going east, to embrace Devon as well, However it has been more than a longer journey in terms of sheer mileage and geography. Psychic paintings, auras, hypnosis and luck — these are only some of the Occult subjects I have explored for the first time. Hopefully, too, I have dug more deeply into aspects like clairvoyancy, healing and the psychic qualities of animals.

And as you travel with me on these Occult journeys across the Westcountry, I hope the cynical will become more tolerant and the believer more open-minded. I shall be content to keep a low profile, content to let people — and events — speak for themselves. Let us start, then, at Exmouth where sad and lonely Lady Nelson lived. But our visit has nothing to do with the Nelsons or Lady Hamilton. It may though have something to do with the Devil himself.

1
The Devil's Footprints
Jane Vansittart at Exmouth

The night of 8 February 1855 was a cruel one and Devon people, who emerged at first light, were amazed. From Totnes to the east of Exmouth they stared in astonishment at the white world: strange, inexplicable footprints tattooed the ground. They marched across farms and gardens, through yards and streets and along lanes and beaches. Some people called them the Devil's Footprints. One witness was Admiral Dobbie, and one hundred and twenty three years on I found myself talking to his grand-daughter about this still unsolved mystery.

Jane Vansittart was born in Exmouth and lives there today, but she has travelled widely, living in Italy, China, Bermuda, Jamaica, the Azores and the United States. The author of eleven books, including six historical novels, she said, 'I was brought up with the story and the whole mystery has fascinated me.' She has in fact, used the Devil's Footprints in a novel entitled *The Devil's Wind,* and over the years has accumulated some very thorough evidence relating to those eerie marks on the landscape.

'All over the snow,' she explained, 'were these clear impressions of a donkey's hooves, four inches long by two and a quarter wide, going in a straight line so that two parallel lines six inches apart could contain them, as if made by a biped. Eight inches lay between each mark, sometimes a little more, but always they lay in a straight line across field and lawn, road and track, woods and common, sometimes over the roofs, houses and hayricks, taking high walls in their unbroken stride. They lay on both sides of rivers, through villages and towns, and in the gardens, covering an area of thirty or forty miles of the coastal belt.

'There were thousands of these marks. They were widespread. They remained in the frozen snow for several days. They caused wonder, fear and surprise. They were attributed to almost everything from a visitation of the Devil, an escaped animal from a Zoo, to an unknown sea monster or the neighbour's cat.

'Hundreds of people of all walks of life, of all ages, and of all intelligences, saw them. Countrymen, gamekeepers, and sportsmen with their knowledge of wild animals and their tracks, could not account for them.

'To this day there is no proven or entirely satisfactory answer, and the field is still open to the naturalist, the psychical researcher, the scientist, or any de-bunker.'

On the 24 February, 1855, the *Illustrated London News* published an account of the occurrence which was written by 'South Devon', the *nom de plume* of Mr Durban of Newport House, Countess Weir, near Exeter. The following is Jane Vansittart's edited version of that wordy article.

'Many of your readers have perused the paragraph which appeared in the papers of last week, relative to the mysterious foot-marks left upon the snow during the night of Thursday the 8th February . . . The marks were to all appearances the perfect impressions of a donkey's hoof, the length of four inches by two and a quarter inches . . . It appeared that foot had followed foot, in a single line, the distance from each tread being eight inches, or rather more in every parish . . . It passed once down or across each garden or courtyard, and did so in nearly all the houses in many parts of the town mentioned, as also in the farms scattered about, the regular tracks passing over the roofs of houses, hayricks, and one fourteen foot wall, without displacing the snow on either side or altering the distance between the feet, and passing on as if the wall had not been any impediment . . .

'Birds could not leave these marks. The effect of the atmosphere upon these tracks is given as a solution, but how could it be possible for the atmosphere to affect one impression and not another? On that morning the snow bore the marks of cats, dogs, rabbits, birds and men clearly defined, why then should this particular mark be the only one which was affected by the atmosphere, and all the others left as they were? Besides the most singular circumstance was that this particular mark removed the snow where ever it appeared, clear, as if cut with a diamond or branded with a hot iron . . .

'The writer of the above has much experience in tracking wild animals and birds upon the snow in the backwoods of Canada, and can safely say he has never seen a more clearly defined track, or one that appeared to be less altered by the atmosphere.

'I send you a copy of the foot, taken in the snow, and also a succession of the steps.'

The Reverend K. Ellecombe of Clyst St George also wrote to the Editor of the *Illustrated London News* on 13 March 1855:

'Without any wish to make myself conspicuous in this interesting enquiry about the Devon snow marks . . . living as I do, in the locality where they appeared, and being myself an eyewitness of some of them . . . I cannot help venturing an opinion.

'There is no doubt as to the facts, that thousands of these marks were seen on the snow on the morning of the 9th February, extending over many miles on either side of the estuaries of the Exe and the Clyst, even to the city. All agree in form, varying a little in size, but the general appearance was the same, that of a donkey's foot. They seem as if the snow had been branded with a hot iron, or the form of such a shoe had been cut out with a knife to the ground, which was everywhere visible, though the snow in the middle part did not appear to be touched.

'The depth (of the snow) was about three quarters of an inch. Snow fell at midnight, then there was sleet and a thaw, and after that a freeze. The night was not dark. The marks of one creature were on my own premises, across a lawn, round the house to a pump shed. These were visible three days afterwards. My dog barked that night, as did the dogs of my neighbours where marks were seen. There is scarcely a field or an orchard or garden where they were not, all in a single line, under hedges, and, in one field near me a turning round and a doubling appeared. The two neighbours who followed the tracks through some fields met with excrement, and there the tracks were spread wider, and doubled, and afterwards single and shaped as before. The excrements were four oblong lobes of a whitish colour the size and shape of a large grape.

'At Exmouth, I have been informed, there were marks in the middle of a field, isolated, without any apparent approach or retreat, and all in one direction, and so they were in many gardens closed with high walls. In one place the marks appeared under a wall to the end of the garden, and then turned round and returned *half the length*. At Marley House next to Exmouth, marks were seen on the sill of a window two stories high.'

Though the footprints have been seen in other places — invariably when snow has fallen — it was not until 1963 that Jane Vansittart obtained eye witness accounts of similar footprints in Devon.

'Why the wide time gap?' I asked her.

'I've no idea,' she admitted, 'and why Devon again? An ancient civilization was here and maybe that has something to do with it. One wonders too what happens when it's not snowing . . . no footprints or invisible footprints there all the time?'

In that bitter winter of 1963 footprints were seen, measured and drawn by two people in Mannamead, and another in Noss Mayo.

'These last descriptions and drawings are identical with those of 1855,' a Mannamead resident told Jane Vansittart. 'During the recent snow I and a friend noticed some very odd prints in the snow. They seemed to be made by an animal such as a donkey. It seemed very peculiar as there were six marks in the drive up to the eight foot high garage, and six more on the grass behind the garage. There is no access to the back from the garage except over the roof. Nothing else marked the snow anywhere. We saw them clearly early in the morning after a night of snow. They were again snowed on. When the thaw started they appeared again, and we again examined them. My garden is not easy to get into by an animal. I have not heard of other reports round here, but doubtless others felt as I did, that it sounded so ridiculous it was better to say nothing.'

On 29 June 1963 Miss Vansittart received a letter from Noss Mayo:

'I had the good fortune to see these prints in a long straight line outside my cottage windows after a new fall of snow, sometime I should say about 8 a.m. My cottage is quite close to a wood. I, like the correspondent you mentioned today, was quite convinced that nobody would believe me so I kept it to myself. At that particular time everybody was more or less housebound, and always during the winter months my circle is a very small one . . . At that same period while having a bath around 8 p.m. I heard a most terrifying howl, the like of which I have never heard before, nor wish to hear again. This howl was not a fox . . . I am sorry I cannot give you the exact date, except that I had become accustomed to the idea of snow . . . as near as possible I should say the first or second week in February . . .

'Two thirds of the block belongs to me, but the footprints went on and past the small one on the end (of the house) making in all quite forty feet. You will see the River Yealm (tidal) runs right along my garden, about half a mile from the estuary . . . I am sorry I cannot send you a sketch. All I can repeat is what I said at first, at a space of about eighteen inches these marks were on this virgin head of snow,

10

I should say about the size of a lady's hand when clenched, along the whole length of these cottages. Will you be kind enough to let me know if and when you find an explanation.'

Both eye witnesses preferred to remain anonymous. Jane Vansittart, however, felt that they were down-to-earth people and saw no reason to question the veracity of their accounts.

She went on: 'These 1963 accounts rule out any question of the 1855 manifestation being either fiction, mass hysteria or wild imagination; so let us now look at the evidence, the explanations and details as furnished in 1855, after the most widespread, the best documented, and most widely observed example of this strange phenomenon. Different theories have been brought forward to explain the footprints.

'High frequency rays from a type of aerial echo sounder from visitors from outer space were suggested.

'Migrating eels were cited. These eels come from the Sargasso Sea and once in a lifetime they migrate back to the sea. Eels are known to make long journeys over land, climbing obstacles in their way. Tiny eels on their arrival in British rivers have been seen to scale sheer, wet rock. But can a full grown eel climb a wall or a house? How then is the horseshoe mark made? With their jaws while travelling in some different way from their usual sinuous movement? Could the short thaw have stimulated an unusual mass migration?

'It has been suggested that the marks are the result of freak weather conditions, such as a current of warm air coming in contact with a very low temperature, setting up condensation which projects water-blobs earthwards to mark the smooth snow. These have been observed in Canada appearing at intervals of seven feet, and producing marks nineteen by fourteen inches running in a single straight line. They have also been seen in a slightly smaller form at Strathspey, Scotland. Again, neither the measurements nor the single line agrees with the 1855 descriptions.

'Long tailed wood mice have been named as the authors of the tracks, but their marks, if the right shape, are smaller than the carefully drawn diagrams of 1855 and of 1963. Furthermore, do these mice ever swarm simultaneously over a large tract of country as in 1855? If such a common animal were responsible would they not have been named with certainty by the hundreds of countrymen who saw them?

'Was it mass migration, a mass immigration, or just an undirected swarm?

'Had there been an obvious explanation, would the long-experienced bailiff of Oxton House, near Kenton, have insisted, in spite of one irascible refusal, that his employer, General Studd, leave his meal and come at once to see the strange marks that crossed the lawn outside his house?

'In the rational age in which we now live a natural explanation is sought. At the same time it is recognised that not all natural laws are fully understood, nor are the laws that govern the atmosphere and outer space. Some day science, or some branch of it, may find an answer to this mystery. In the meantime one can only watch and wait for another manifestation. Next time let us hope that a camera is on hand, loaded with film, and that a naturalist, a physicist, a psychic researcher, and several scientists are within call. Anyone of them may be needed!'

Patrick Moore, who has carefully read Miss Vansittart's file, told her, 'I do congratulate you on assembling all the information so well. The trouble is that when I had finished it, I thought that the mystery was probably deeper than ever, and I am as far from a solution as I was at the outset . . . which is a tribute to, not a criticism of, your own compilation! We have here a real mystery story which is more real than anything in Agatha Christie.'

I asked Miss Vansittart if she had drawn any conclusions.

'The more I have researched,' she said, 'the less idea I have. It's clearly some phenomenon which we don't understand and I don't mean little green men at the bottom of the garden. It's an utter mystery and though I have feelings about places and am sensitive to atmosphere, I'm not particularly Occult-minded. No known animal would walk in a straight line or leap these high walls.

'I've got evidence . . . plenty of evidence but not one single part of an explanation . . .'

2
Clairvoyancy

Acora at the Barbican

'I'm not a God. There are times when my predictions are wrong or don't work out as I expect them to. If I could see everything, I'd be Jesus Christ. Eighty per cent . . . or more . . . of my predictions come true. I tell people bad things too. Otherwise I'd be just another sea-side fortune teller. But I can't predict for my wife or myself . . . or for those who are close to me.'

The sandy-haired young man, sitting opposite me, was Acora, the Westcountry's leading Romany clairvoyant.

Those penetrating eyes moved from me to the crystal ball lying on the low circular wooden table, divided into astrological patterns. 'I use the crystal as a tool of the trade,' he explained. 'Some people think you see pictures in it, but you don't. I use it to clear my mind. Looking into this ball of nothing helps you to concentrate on the subject, and you start picking up messages. It's difficult to put it into words because you don't actually see things. You feel things happening; and you can help some people more than others. With some you feel a kind of brick-wall going up, almost as if they're afraid of you, or maybe they're just afraid of what you are going to tell them.

'Yes, I am very conscious of my responsibilities. There was one young woman who came in, and I saw that her husband was not in love with her, that he was having an affair with another woman. I *had* to tell her. She attempted to commit suicide when she discovered, from her husband, that I had been telling nothing but the truth. Then there was a woman, one of my great supporters, who came to me, saying her husband was dying of cancer, that the doctors could do nothing for him. ''Come and heal him,'' she begged, ''lay your Romany hands on him and you'll save him.'' I was her last hope . . . it was pathetic . . . of course, I couldn't. I'm not a healer. The husband died, and she's never been to see me again.

'Things like that don't tire you. They age you. They're like somebody putting a great weight on my head.

'But then there are times when you feel wonderful. This woman came to me; she'd been to see the top specialists but they all told her the same thing — she couldn't have any children. I predicted they would be wrong. When I next heard from her, she told me she had given birth to two boys!'

Acora wears large gold rings. His hands are rarely still. He talks at close range, somehow making you feel you're the only person in the world. The words cascade like water from a fountain. It is a surprise to learn that he had a very broken education, and wouldn't pass a simple academic examination. He speaks at great speed, but with great intensity — and his sensitive hands gesticulate when he wishes to add emphasis to a point.

Technically he uses four methods of prediction: reading the crystal ball, reading tarot cards, palmistry — reading of the hand — and clairvoyancy. 'To me, clairvoyancy is the real test of predictions. Anybody can buy a book and learn how to read cards or hands after a fashion. But clairvoyancy is a real Romany gift. That sorts out the people who claim to be able to tell and those who *can*. Clear seeing — that's what I call it. And then, of course, all of us who try and look into the future depend on Astrology, the position of the stars at the date and time of a man or woman's birth . . . they're important.

'Some people think predictions are only good for a laugh. Well, I'm not one of them. Reading character and looking into the future — for me — are serious matters. I only laugh about the subject when I hear of horoscopes by computer. Clairvoyancy is a very personal thing. I just don't believe machines — however expensive they are or how many gadgets they have — can give the very personal service that a clairvoyant can give. Of course, there are good and bad clairvoyants. I ask only to be judged by my results.

'Quite a few famous people have come to see me. There's nothing strange about this. Kings and emperors have used clairvoyants. Even Queen Victoria had one.

'I come from a long line of Romany gypsies. My great grandmother was Madam Zambra, whose clients included royalty. Real clairvoyancy is a Romany inheritance, something handed down the ages, from generation to generation. Occasionally it'll miss a generation, but it's something in the blood.

'It was my grandmother who recognised that I had the gift. They tell me I was about three or four and the family were out in the

14

country, somewhere in the wilds of Dartmoor. It was a hot summer's day and I said I wanted an ice cream, but my father explained you wouldn't find an ice-cream parlour or even a van in a place like that. ''Go down the hill, and turn right,'' I told him. Maybe just to keep me quiet, they went down the hill and turned right, and there, coming up the road, was an ice-cream van. Immediately my grandmother knew I had the gift.'

This second Occult journey had brought me back over the Tamar into Devon again. We were talking in his consulting room at the Barbican, that lovely old Elizabethan part of Plymouth, by the waterside — up a quaint cobbled street, oddly enough called New Street. Drake and Raleigh and the other great Westcountry seadogs once walked this way — and more recently Sir Francis Chichester who invariably began and ended his voyages here at Plymouth. Acora's consulting room, at no. 45a, stands by an old Jewish cemetery. You turn up a narrow alleyway into a tiny courtyard and garden — 'my secret garden' he calls it.

Photographs of famous show business personalities surrounded us: Mike and Bernie Winters, Larry Grayson, dancer Lionel Blair, Tommy Cooper, Kathy Kirby, Des O'Connor and Bob Monkhouse among others. Acora finds it quite natural that celebrities should use his services. 'King Arthur had Merlin. Hitler had an astrologer, though he didn't go and see him towards the end of the war. Churchill must have been a clairvoyant. He *saw* the war coming. He *saw* how the war was developing : how we were going to have trouble with the Russians after it.'

About ten years ago, Acora met Enoch Powell, then one of the leaders of the Conservative Party, possibly a future Conservative Prime Minister. 'You're going to change sides,' Acora told him. It was ludicrous, of course, and Powell just smiled. But today Powell no longer sits among his old Tory colleagues. He sits as an Ulster Unionist — something few political pundits would have ever contemplated.

A fascinating local prediction was that concerning Louise Churchill. Some years ago Louise was a make-up artist with Westward Television at Derry's Cross. She recalls: 'Acora came to the Westward studios to do a programme on clairvoyancy. I had met him before, and during the meal break we sat together. It was then that he said to me, ''You'll not be here for very much longer. You'll change your job and will become well known in this area.'' At the time I had no intention of leaving Westward and Plymouth Sound had not even been formed as a Company.' Today Louise has her own programme on Plymouth Sound. Looking back to that lunchtime four calendars ago, she says, 'It does seem a remarkably accurate piece of clairvoyancy!'

Then there was the case of Lesley Russ, a Plymouth-born girl who had gone to London to become a photographer's model. A complete cynic, she had never before been to a clairvoyant. But back in Plymouth, she heard of Acora's talents and made an appointment at The Barbican. Gazing into his crystall ball, talking to her across that same circular table, he predicted success and saw her travelling overseas before settling down. Settling down, he said, would come with a lightning romance. 'She thought it sounded too fantastic to be true. Well, she went to the four corners of the world. Then she met her husband-to-be, a wealthy stockbroker, the day after she got back to England from a trip to Europe and they were married inside a month. Lesley's mother only just made the wedding. I'd seen it all coming.'

Acora himself married his very attractive wife, Jeannette, back in 1974. It was a wedding Plymouth is not likely to forget. Forty gypsy caravans were parked outside the Parish church at Plympton, and later his three-hundred and fifty guests went to the City Guildhall for the reception. Had he seen his own marriage coming?

'Not really. I just cannot see these things for myself.'

Acora and Jeannette live in a modern Romany caravan in summer. Drawn by a car, it travels vast distances, following various fairs like Corpus Christi at Penzance, May Day at Padstow, Widecombe Fair on Dartmoor, Tavistock Goose Fair, and as far afield as Bridgwater in Somerset. During the winter months, the car and 'the waggon' reside in Cornwall. 'I'd die if I had to live permanently in a house,' Acora admitted. 'If somebody said "No more waggon; you've got to live in a house . . . any house, for ever" they could start making my coffin, start driving the nails in. It's this Romany wanderlust.

'I am unlike some clairvoyants,' says Acora, 'who simply dish out a string of golden predictions. They concentrate on only the good things, and gloss over the bad. Well, that's not my style. When people need it, they get the gypsy's warning.'

'Gypsy's warning' is an expression almost as old as the hills. One man, who hastily heeded an Acora warning, was TV and stage star

1. **The Merry Maidens near Lamorna: '. . . they started trying to uproot one of the stones when the lead horse suddenly dropped dead.'**

2.   Acora with poet, Pam Ayres, at Plymouth Sound.

3. Acora: 'Looking into this ball . . . you start picking up
messages.'

4. Barras Head near Tintagel: 'Tex always halted. Nothing would induce him to go on . . .'

5.   Rough Tor: 'On top of Rough Tor he hid in a crevice and refused to go another inch. He shook like a seriously ill animal.

6. 'Did Tex, then, detect something beyond our vision?'
7. Merlin's Cave Tintagel: 'I felt a tremendous pressure on
my head and my heart started racing as I entered
the cave.'

8. Rex: 'He showed a good deal of caution on entering the cave.'

9.   St Nectan's Glen near Tintagel: 'The most haunted glen in Cornwall.'

10.   Jeannette and star comedian, Larry Grayson.

Larry Grayson. During the summer of 1976, the comedian with the famous 'Shut that Door!' catchphrase, was starring in a show entitled *Larry Grayson's Scandals* at the Princess Theatre, Torquay. One morning, in mid-season, Larry Grayson had an hour-long consultation with Acora. Less than seventy-two hours later the comedian was gravely telling the press he had cancelled an Australian tour — that would have earned him a six figure sum — because of the clairvoyant's warning.

Acora, without a shred of prior knowledge, forecast that Larry was planning an Australian trip and advised him to cancel it. The comedian immediately contacted his management and called off the trip. 'My TV shows have done well there,' he said. 'They love me over there. But I'm a firm believer in the stars and Acora told me so many accurate things about my private life, I was amazed. I didn't hesitate to follow his advice about the Australian tour. I can always tell within three minutes if a clairvoyant is any good. If they're not, I tell them to stop wasting my time. But Acora is undoubtedly gifted.'

Acora says, 'I seem to be able to pick up vibrations very quickly, often within only minutes of meeting someone. For example, early in 1976, I was at the HTV studios in Bristol and there — for the first time — I met TV presenter Jan Leeming. I told her she would be leaving Bristol and that she would be breaking into national television. Frankly, I'm not sure that Jan believed me. Anyway around the fall of the leaves, one day, I was sitting in front of the TV set, when suddenly Jan Leeming appeared on the screen, presenting the very popular Pebble Mill programme. Jan had joined the BBC, had left Bristol — and had made the national breakthrough I'd seen months before. I can see a lot more success ahead for Jan. She's charming and talented, and very interested in the Occult.

'Perhaps even more oddly I can make predictions without meeting people. On New Year's Day 1976, the BBC asked me to make some predictions for the coming year, and that day, in front of their cameras, I indicated a change in the leadership of the Labour Party and the Government. The interesting thing is that I know next to nothing about politics and had never met Harold Wilson. Yet within less than four months, Harold Wilson was out of No. 10 Downing Street, and Jim Callaghan was in — something no political commentator had hinted at in the January of that year.

'Both in my work as a clairvoyant and a personal problem consultant, I have come to the conclusion that most people prefer an anonymous Romany as a Father Confessor. Once upon a time, they would probably have consulted their family doctor or the parish priest. But today the doctors are too busy; while the churches get emptier and emptier. When I was a boy, travelling up and down the lanes and roads of the Westcountry with my grandparents, we depended on signposts. Well, today, as both clairvoyant and adviser, I've become a kind of human signpost. Fact is many people, who consult me, seem to have lost their way in Life, and I like to think I am able to help them to find their bearings — and perhaps themselves.'

I asked him about the Romany race. Their beginnings, it seems, are lost in the mists of time.

'Some say we are descendants of a special caste of Hindus. Others say we originated from Egypt. Look at the word ''Egypt'' — cover the E and you've got ''gypt''.

'Whatever the date, and whatever the route, we, Romany folk, brought age-old wisdom, superstition, and the ability to foretell. Our second sight comes from no computer or scientific juggling. Ours is a true Romany inheritance — a gift from Nature.'

Like the Jews, the gypsies though were victims of Hitler's fanaticism, and thousands perished in concentration camps: a cruel, ironic fate engineered by a man who depended heavily on astrologers.

'Happily, my earliest memories have no such chambers of horror. I recall travelling along the lonely lanes and roads of Cornwall and Devon with my grandmother. In the winter months, we visited villages and isolated farms and cottages, deep in the heart of the Cornish countryside, hawking things like pins and needles, lace and cotton — and, of course, telling fortunes. Gran always carried her crystal ball.

'In the summer, she followed the fairs and the carnivals. And in the days when my grandfather was alive, they had a pot waggon, drawn by a horse, with pots and pans dangling from the sides of the waggon. Grandfather would ring his handbell to bring the people out of their homes.

'As a boy I can vividly remember going to a Romany gathering at Christmas, when the trailers made a circle around a tap-dancing board. A fiddler played alongside a man with a squeeze-box. A fire burnt brightly as the dancers moved rhythmically to the tunes under a star-studded sky. Old men and women gossiped. Women, with their gold sovereign earrings pierced through their ears, wore dresses that stretched to the ground. Old men smoked pipes almost as old as themselves. It were as if you had stepped back in time.

'We did many hawking expeditions around the Westcountry villages in December. I'd pick moss from the moors; get holly and make holly wreaths for the market stalls. Then about four days before Christmas, I'd go from door to door, selling mistletoe. As for Gran, she usually came back with the same amount of lace she'd set out with. She earned most of her money from the crystal ball hidden in her basket.

'So you can see I come from true travelling Romany stock.

'Some Romany people, today, have turned their backs on the traditional ways and have become successful in business. I'm perhaps an exception to the rule — in that I earn my living with the crystal ball.

'We, Romany folk, are very proud of our ancient language. Many of the older travelling folk treated it as something to be closely guarded, looking upon it as a secret language. Now gypsies speak a mixture of English and Romanish. My wife Jeannette and I, when we're together, use a lot of Romanish in our conversation. You can even add up in Romanish.

'When we meet someone we invariably say: "Sar shin" which is "How are you?"

'Most of you live in a house, which we call a "kenner". I live in a trailer which, according to Romany people, is "vardo". Sometimes we have a "yog" outside the "vardo" — a fire outside the trailer.

'When I end a letter, I usually sign off "Kooshti Duker" which means "Good fortune".'

I first met Acora in September 1975. By the November of that year we had completed his first publication *Gypsy Horoscope*. In the preface, I wrote: 'The predictions and character readings in this *Gypsy Horosope* are entirely Acora's. He enjoyed only a broken education — typical in fact of many Romany people — and he does not regard himself as a literary man. In the case of the following pages, he has talked to me and I have put his thoughts and words to paper. Furthermore, he has vetted all that this publication contains. We therefore ask you to regard this Horoscope as a gypsy's spoken word — and not to judge it as a written work.

'In that sense Acora is the real author.'

Gypsy Horoscope's success — we sold over seven thousand copies — encouraged us to publish a follow-up entitled *You & Your Future*, and between the appearance of the two publications, we became business partners, starting a postal horoscope service that was soon attracting clients from as far as Australia and the United States, Acora providing the character analysis and predictions, and I merely acting as a kind of messenger, putting his deep thoughts to paper.

Then our collaboration took on another dimension one Friday lunchtime when we met John Theobald, the then Editorial Director of *The Independent*, in a Barbican bar. He suggested a personal problem column by Acora in the newspaper each Sunday. As with horoscopes, we resolved to keep the service strictly confidential and therefore never reveal the identity of the people who write and even occasionally we alter the geography slightly to conceal identification.

Initially, I was surprised by the curiously aggressive attitude of some Church people towards Acora and the subject of clairvoyancy in general.

The tone of many was captured in a letter Acora received from one young lady. She wrote: 'Dear Acora, I'm deeply in love, and want to know if this relationship will lead to a happy marriage. I would very much like to go to a clairvoyant, but, as a regular church member, my church friends tell me that consulting a clairvoyant is totally wrong. Is this so?'

Acora replied: 'Constantly I come across this problem. Frankly I can never understand why the Church takes such a negative attitude about predictions, especially when the Bible itself is littered with so many.

'Were not the wise men guided to the baby Jesus by a star? Did not John say that the appearance of Christ confirmed the prophecy? Wasn't Christ himself constantly predicting in his sermons?

'I promise you that you'll find more predictions inside the pages of the Bible than in any modern horoscope publication — and I say that reverently and sincerely. Why you'll even find sections of the Bible with headings like ''The Book of the Prophet Jeremiah''.

'Christians have been involved with the prediction business for something like two thousand years, and that's why I'm mystified by the Church's curiously negative attitude about clairvoyancy. Some Church people almost imply that by consulting a clairvoyant you're consorting with the Devil!

'I don't take that pagan line. Indeed I regard my gift of second sight as Heaven-sent. I make no pretence about possessing a Godlike quality, but I believe that it's only right and proper that I should use that talent to the best of my ability.

28

'Is there not a parable in the Good Book about employing our individual talents?

'No, young lady, you'll suffer no harm through consulting a reputable clairvoyant. Of course, there are charlatans in this field, as there are in any professional field — including the Church. Have you seen those religious characters, parading up and down the streets, waving banners with warnings like ''Prepare to Meet Thy Doom''. If I did that, I should almost certainly be locked up.

'Despite what your church friends say, if you decide to consult a clairvoyant, I predict that you'll be surprised . . . and helped.'

This published reply, however, provoked another barrage of critical letters. So much so that Acora, on my suggestion, devoted the whole column the following Sunday to answering some of the points raised by his critics.

'First I would like to stress that personally I have no argument with the Church,' he said. 'I have counted it a pleasure to attend church fetes — as a professional clairvoyant — and help to raise money for their various causes.

'Secondly, I cannot understand why some people are mystified when I say that I regard my gift of clairvoyancy as Heaven-sent and yet still employ things like the crystal and tarot cards.

'As I see it, the painter too has been given another kind of vision. But he cannot produce his pictures without paint, brushes and canvas. These are the tools of his calling. Likewise, I need my tools. Though I don't actually see pictures when I look into the crystal, this does, in fact, help to clear my mind, enables me to concentrate and give the person concerned a better reading.

'My mail bag also included one long, very angry letter from a church lady who says I am destined to be flung into the sea with a millstone round my neck for practising clairvoyancy. I will overlook the fact that the lady herself is indulging in a little clairvoyancy! Frankly, I don't think her words either very kind or very Christian. Indeed, I would be ashamed to make such a prediction. Furthermore, if I used such language, there would be allegations of consorting with the Devil.

'I was also disturbed by the twisting of words in certain letters. I was told, more than once, that words spoken by Jesus Christ were not really predictions.

'Now I'm no Biblical scholar, and I'm always willing to learn and to be corrected. But I'm sticking to my view that the Bible is the

greatest horoscope book of all time. When, for example, Christ said
he would die, but rise again — if that isn't a prediction, I don't know
what is.

'At the other end of the scale, there were very sincere church
people, who wrote in, saying I should advise people to pray to God
instead of consulting a clairvoyant.

'I respect their point of view, but the snag here is that many of the
people who consult me do not believe in a God of any kind. Telling
them to speak or pray — into a great emptiness (as it seems to them)
would be cruel and pointless. Quite a few even no longer believe in
themselves, and here I like to think I am able to help them to get back
a measure of self-confidence.

'Finally, some of my clients are regular worshippers. More than
one vicar has come to me for consultation, and among my possess-
ions is a letter from a well-known Westcountry parson — to a lady
with a problem — advising her to come and see me.

We both took encouragement from a lady in Newquay who wrote
'I'm proud of my Church membership *and* I'm proud of my friend-
ship with Acora; though I may be one of his clients I still think of him
as a friend. Acora saved me from suicide and has given me the will to
go on living.'

Acora luckily has the strength of character to rise above peevish
criticism. 'I've been under constant attack since the age of seven,
when I first started making predictions,' he says. 'If my predictions
don't work out as people want, some of them call me a charlatan; and
if my forecasts do work out, they dismiss it all as a coincidence! So,
in a way, I can't win!

'Clairvoyancy, somehow somewhere along the line got confused
with witchcraft. Maybe it's due to the fact that in the old days some
fortune tellers abused the privilege of confidential information. A
woman might come to a fortune-teller and confess that she was
having ''an affair'' with a married man. Consequently she might find
herself being blackmailed. This is why today someone like myself is
not allowed to join the Guild of Showmen. We, presentday clairvoyants, are having to pay this unfair price for wrong deeds, generations
back in time.

'And here I'd like to take the opportunity of saying that all people
— who contact me either in the flesh or by letter — can do so in the
safe knowledge that I treat all consultations in the strictest confidence.

30

'Not long ago, I visited Boscastle, that lovely village up on the North Cornish coast, and heard how years ago Sir Henry Irving, the famous actor-manager, came there on holiday. His visit to Boscastle apparently coincided with a time when his fortunes were going through a bad patch. So he went to a Boscastle witch and asked her if she would unwind the bad spell through which he was travelling.

'Sir Henry's fortunes did recover. The cynic, of course, would merely dismiss it as ''just a coincidence''.

'As I said, I hear that sort of remark all the time.

'However, that was the positive good side of the Occult employed by the wise woman of Boscastle . . . and I like to think it is this same good positive spirit I bring into my work as a clairvoyant today.'

3
Luck

Madam Jeannette at Gunnislake

Everyone hopes to be lucky.

Luck is a mysterious something — like a pot of gold at the end of the rainbow — something that most of us look for or hope for. Buddhists, Christians and Atheists may have next to nothing in common, but they all acknowledge that most elusive of the Goddesses — Lady Luck.

I have always been fascinated by luck since captaining a cricket touring team back in the late 1950s. We played ten matches, and I won the toss for ten days running, every day calling 'Tails'. I never again called 'Heads'.

Jeannette Broadway, wife of Acora, the Romany clairvoyant, ventured into the horoscope business in 1977 with a whole series of Zodiac messages, published under the general title of *Your Luck & Life* by Madame Jeannette.

Who better then to talk about luck in life?

'I firmly believe in luck,' she said, 'and I believe everybody else does too. Even those who won't admit it . . .' She is a totally different interviewee from her husband. Darkly sun-tanned — an impression intensified against the blue and white she was wearing, the words came slowly, quietly, almost carefully. We were talking in their modern caravan, 'trailers' as travellers call them. Outside it was a blazing July afternoon: a bright blue sky with temperatures in the eighties, and everywhere the scent of summer.

'I also believe in lucky breaks and streaks,' she went on. 'A football team may be playing brilliant football, but still not score the goals, and lose their matches; all a question of the run of the ball, and you're back to luck. And the same with show business, you've lots of people competing for the star spots, and often it's a question of being spotted by the right person at the right moment, and once more you're back to luck.

'Of course, some people moan about their lack of luck. They almost think that luck is going to come and find them. It's the same as people who come to be 'dukkered' — Romanish for fortune telling — many think that because a certain prediction is made, all they have to do is sit back and it'll just happen. But Life isn't like that.

'It's a question of co-operating with Fate. It's a question of effort too. Somebody might, for example, say that Angela Rippon has been lucky to have gone so far in the television world . . . a world which until now was dominated by men. OK, Angela Rippon may have been lucky in time, in the sense that she is about at a time when the mood is changing. But she's very professional, and has worked very, very hard to get to the top. I don't think she'd say it was just all luck, and I don't think it's just all luck either. It's a combination of luck and effort.

'I met Larry Grayson, the star comedian, when he was doing a summer season at Torquay. He told me something about his struggle to get to the top . . . years and years of slogging away in clubs for poor pay . . . and then suddenly he was spotted, changed his style of comedy, and now he's top of the bill and one of the best-paid comedians in the business with his chauffeur-driven white Rolls. A real professional . . . again a mixture of hard work and making the most of his chance when it came.'

There is a German saying which goes: 'Luck follows the hopeful, ill luck the fearful.' And that belief is not irrational when you think of Jung, the celebrated Swiss psychologist, who evolved a theory called 'Synchronicity' in which he put forward the idea that a person's psychological condition attracts events to him or her. If a person feels lucky, in reality they stand more chance of being lucky. And, of course, logically the reverse applies.

Now though Jeannette had no pretence about understanding the complexities of psychology, she readily agreed: 'If a man or a woman feels lucky, the odds are they'll attract luck. In fact, I'd say luck is largely a matter of feelings. I wouldn't know how to define luck, but I know when I'm feeling lucky. I might be playing cards or am at bingo, and I feel when I'm on a lucky streak. Also I'll often know when to stop, when the winning streak is about to end.'

I suddenly remembered the old belief that if a hunchback crosses your path, you may expect a continuation of good luck or even a change for the better. Time was when the Monte Carlo casino employed a hunchback for this very reason. Whenever a successful gambler was about to leave the table with his rich harvest of winnings, the hunchback was ordered to put in an appearance: the strategy of the casino being that this might tempt the successful gambler into trying his hand once more — believing that the 'winning streak' was still with him — and, of course, hoping that he would lose all he had won.

So naturally our conversation moved to lucky numbers. Jeannette, like her husband, is of Romany blood; this, allied to her knowledge of the Zodiac, enables her to recommend lucky numbers to people, depending on their date of birth. 'By ancient lore,' Jeannette said, 'the various signs of the Zodiac have a lucky number. For example, if you're say Aries, the first sign of the Zodiac, your Romany lucky number is 7. Here I would recommend you to make important dates or engagements for the 7th day of the week or the month, when influences would usually be in your favour; July, the 7th month in the calendar, too, will often prove to be a good time for the Aries subject.

'Decisions made in the region of 7 o'clock would usually be sound ones, and addresses, incorporating the number 7, will often be of significance to the Aries subject. And, of course, if a flutter were being considered, horse no. 7 or a ticket number somehow involved with 7, will usually do well for you.'

'What about the other Zodiac signs?' I asked.

'Well,' Jeannette explained, 'if you're Taurus, the second sign in the Zodiac, your Romany lucky number is 8, and you'd be wise to work along the same lines. For Gemini subjects it's 2, their Zodiac symbol is double . . . the heavenly twins. Cancer's 5 and Leo's 1. Then you go to Virgo, the Virgin, and it's 4 which is rated one of the luckiest numbers of all . . . think of the four elements: Air, Earth, Fire and Water. Now we go into the second half of the Zodiac; for Libra it's 6; for Scorpio, my husband's sign, it's 9. Then Sagittarius — my own sign — is 6. Capricorn is 5. Aquarius, your sign, that's 4 and finally Pisces that's 3.

'But that's all according to tradition,' Jeannette continued. 'I think people can find their own lucky number. I, for example, have had a lot of good luck with number 13 which most people rate an unlucky number. I've had some very successful days on the 13th of the month, even on Friday 13th. Actually I like Friday as a day . . . and I don't know why . . . yes, maybe because it's the eve of some of our biggest Fairs.'

From Romany lucky numbers, our thoughts went on to colours.

'Personally, I don't rely on one particular colour for luck. I choose the colour according to my mood, but there is an old Romany belief that certain colours will bring certain people good luck. My husband's Scorpio; well red is the colour for that sign of the Zodiac, and when he's appearing on television he always wears a red Romany cravat. Once I said; "You can't wear that, it's dirty." But no; he insisted on wearing it.

'Red's also the colour for Aries; it's said to be an ambitious colour. Taurus's colour is blue — that's rated a very spiritual colour. Gemini is yellow . . . you'll find Gemini subjects among the smartest of the Zodiac.Then violet and ice blue, they're traditionally lucky colours for Cancer. Leo's is gold. Virgo ideally is a combination light grey and brown. Navy blue is Libra . . . Margaret Thatcher, who's Libra, ought to wear plenty of that around election times! Scorpio, as I said, is red; and my own Sagittarian colour, according to this tradition, is purple . . . an interesting thing here is when we were deciding the colouring for the lettering on my Zodiac envelopes, I chose purple, and only when we saw the finished product — how good they looked — did I remember that purple was my lucky colour according to the Romanies . . . well, it worked that time! Capricorn's colours are dark blue and blue; though Capricornians can be quite severe in their styles, they have the knack of making their clothes look expensive. Then we come to the end of the Zodiac with turquoise the Romany colour for Aquarius and sea-green for Pisces.'

The word superstition comes from the old Latin *superstites* meaning survivors, and, to my mind, that's very significant, for superstitions are truly the survivors of bygone ages. They're a mixture of remnants of old religions and beliefs — and magical ritual.

I asked Jeannette if she were superstitious.

'Yes,' she admitted, 'maybe not as much as Acora, but I don't walk under ladders if I can help it or pass people on the stairs. If I'm in a big store and *have* to pass people on the stairs, then I always make sure I cross my fingers as I pass them.

'I'm also very superstitious about not liking to hear certain words, for they always seem to bring bad luck.' For example, she never refers to a certain vermin by their real name, only as 'long tails'.

We then talked about omens for good luck.

'We, Romanies, always like to see a white horse . . . that stands for good luck. It was interesting with Acora's first publication *Gypsy Horoscope* how we went to Chudleigh for the photographing of the cover . . . the setting was a gypsy caravan . . . and suddenly the owner brought out a white horse. That was pure Fate; not planned in any way, and right away we knew it was a good omen.

'And it's interesting to look back on the time when we were working on the first edition of my own *Your Luck & Life* at St Teath, and I looked up and there was a white horse looking over the fence at us . . . that too was a good omen.

'Another thing I like to see is straw travelling on the road. We have an old saying: "See hay money today. See straw money to draw." If I see straw or hay on the road I always say "Kooshti Bok", which is Romanish for good luck and spit on my hands.'

From primitive times spittle has been regarded as a psychic force. An angler spits on his bait, and many street traders spit on the first coin they take at the beginning of the day, believing it will accelerate business.

Jeannette also likes to see a black cat. 'If one crosses my path, I always put a wish on it. I suppose superstition is largely a matter of how you've been brought up. My father believed in luck; if he met a flock of sheep on the road . . . he'd go home. He believed they meant that business wouldn't be any good that day. He also had a way of deliberately trying to break a run of bad luck. I remember we were in Wales once, and day after day he wasn't able to land any jobs, and then one evening he said: "Tomorrow, I'll do a job, even if I lose money on it" . . . and he went out and quoted a price like £10 when he knew it was going to cost him £20. But he did it, believing that the taking of the money would break the ice . . . and it did. He had marvellous work after that for something like three months.'

'What do you think of the old English proverb that it's better to be born lucky than rich?'

She looked thoughtful but had no hesitation: 'I think it's dead right. I've known rich people who were absolutely bombed out . . . not lucky at all . . . making the mistake that they think they can buy their friends. You see them, they sometimes have two, even three marriages, and still don't find happiness. Wealth certainly doesn't necessarily buy happiness.'

'Though you say you can't define luck, can you recognise it?' Her brown eyes looked thoughtful again. 'Yes, I think I can. You feel happy and excited on the inside and yet you're contented at the same time . . . it's a strange mixture and it probably all adds up or boils down to personal happiness.'

4
Are Animals Psychic?

The question has long intrigued me.

Looking back on my own Supernatural experience at Bossiney at midnight on Midsummer Eve 1965, which I told in *Supernatural in Cornwall*, I still vividly recall the sudden personality change in our tan and white rough-haired terrier, Tex. Normally a pugnacious character, courage, that night, suddenly inexplicably deserted him.

I remember, too, setting out early one September morning with Tex and photographer, Bryan Russell, for Brown Willy and Rough Tor. The two highest hills in Cornwall, they stand on Bodmin Moor, one of the wildest landscapes in all the county. Tex ruined the morning. Tail down, eyes mirroring first distrust, then something akin to fear itself, he made a pathetic figure. On top of Rough Tor, he hid in a crevice and refused to go another inch. He shook like a seriously ill animal, and my concern was such that I had no hesitation in abandoning our expedition. Brown Willy, away in the distance, had a majestic, beckoning quality that morning as the sun rimmed the skyline and the haze dissolved; but we started back down the hill towards Rough Tor Farm and the car. I was already contemplating a visit to the veterinary surgeon at Camelford as I carried Tex — a four-legged bundle of tension — down the sloping shoulder of Rough Tor. Halfway down, however, Tex started struggling for his feet. Carefully I placed him on the turf. He scampered away immediately: a different dog. Something high on the roof of Cornwall had disturbed him. Neither Bryan Russell nor myself had a clue. Even today we are none the wiser.

Did Tex, then, detect something beyond our vision? Certainly that September morning when Tex behaved so strangely, I knew next to nothing about Charlotte Dymond, an attractive eighteen-year-old servant girl who had died nearby on a Sunday afternoon in 1844. For ten days there was no sign of the girl, who could neither read nor write. Then a group of local men found her body in a pit by the stream at Rough Tor Ford. She was lying on her back, her throat slashed.

Also on that September morning, with Tex, I knew nothing of claims that Charlotte's ghost had been seen in the vicinity. Later I learned that sentries of the Old Volunteers, camping nearby, swore they saw her walking nightly, over the moor, down the hill and up to the gate into the field where she had died.

Was it Charlotte's ghost perhaps that worried Tex?

I have stood before her grave in Davidstow Churchyard and wondered if the dog had caught a glimpse of her that morning — or the atmosphere of that bloody Sunday afternoon.

But getting back to the dog's strange behaviour on Rough Tor, some people have dismissed the matter in one word: 'Foxes!' I, though, am not prepared to accept that simple theory. Fact is, Tex was no stranger to wildlife or livestock — or eerie landscapes. He had travelled with me on horse rides across Exmoor, occasions when we had come close to grazing stags, and he had shown no anxiety. Yet interestingly, on certain other occasions, his personality had changed radically. I once visited a house near Rock where a murder had been committed, spending some time in the room where the killing had taken place. Personally I found it a perfectly normal bedroom in a perfectly normal house. But Tex was agitated. Whining and moving anxiously from room to room, he only settled when he leapt into the car and I drove off.

Oddly, though, Tex behaved quite normally in what I regard as the most haunted glen in all Cornwall. St Nectan's Glen, a lovely wooded stretch of land with a running stream, lies roughly halfway between Tintagel and Boscastle. Many are the stories concerning St Nectan, and the hermitage and glen that took his name. The chanting of monks at night; invisible sobbing, mocking, inexplicable laughter from an invisible person; beautiful organ music from an empty building; the appearances and sudden disappearances of a strange monklike figure — these are only some of the serious Supernatural claims about St Nectan's Glen. But Tex always behaved normally there.

Yet, in contrast, he behaved apprehensively in a part of North Cornwall with no haunted reputation. In our years at the hotel at Bossiney, we sometimes took the delightful walk down Bossiney Lane, out on to the cliffs and on to Barras Head, the site of an earthwork far older than Tintagel Castle. A path snakes its way along the cliffs and out to the aged headland — Barras Nose the locals call it. Here — at one point — Tex always halted. Nothing would induce him to go on, not even the bribery of a biscuit. Once more some people said: 'Foxes.' But I was less sure, for the pattern persisted during all four seasons. Whatever the time of day, at this precise point, for something like ten yards, Tex, the independent terrier that he was, allowed me to carry him. Then he would struggle for the freedom of his feet. And on the return journey, we would go through the same performance.

Coincidence?

I find one of the most tantalising coincidences that relating to the death of Arthur Piper, a kennelman with the Dartmoor Hunt. He broke his neck on the moor, riding a horse called Silver Fox. He lingered in the thing we call Life for some weeks, and after he died his ashes were placed on a stone on Foxtor, that famous landmark on the great wilderness of Dartmoor. The following week — during a Dartmoor hunt — both fox and hounds ran over the very stone!

Another death — this time relating to an animal — came to me from Betty Hill of Penzance. Down in West Cornwall beyond Lamorna stand the Merry Maidens and the Pipers. They were the men who made the music for the dancing girls — and for the sin of making merry on a Sunday they were turned into stone — that's the legend. These stones are the most famous Cornish circle and Betty Hill has a crystal-clear memory from her childhood concerning them. 'It was the first war, and the Landlord ordered the field to be ploughed, and they started trying to uproot one of the stones when the lead horse suddenly dropped dead. The whole thing was called off, and everybody started crossing themselves.'

Just one more coincidence or further proof that the Supernatural stretches to the animal kingdom?

Since writing *Supernatural in Cornwall,* I have had one incredibly interesting follow-up story.

Mrs Pat Forster of Kennford, Exeter, became very worried about her pet rabbit. 'It got ill and deteriorated badly over a period of two days, with some kind of enteritis. It wouldn't eat anything and was so weak it couldn't stand up or even lift its head. I was at my wits' end to know what to do, so I tried to make contact with someone who could help, using a photo of you from *Supernatural in Cornwall* as a means of establishing contact.' Thus wrote the rabbit's owner to Marilyn Preston, a spiritual healer, who lives at Higher Port View, Saltash. 'The photo seemed to move momentarily . . . and I had a good feeling, and I just knew that the rabbit would get better. Within half an hour it was eating again and by the end of the day it was 100 per cent better. Since then it has grown to be the healthiest, happiest rabbit you've ever seen. I suppose it was a bit of a cheek, Lyn, using your photo in that way, as, for one thing, I'm not sure if you have suffered any feelings of depletion as a result . . . Of course, rabbits *do* suddenly get better, but we were all astonished at the speed of recovery — that was definitely paranormal.'

I asked Marilyn Preston how she accounted for this channelling of healing power through the photograph in the book.

'I'm not as yet sure,' she admitted, 'but feel it could be one of two or three theories. Pat being on my wavelength — an animal lover, a near-vegetarian, an accepter of space friends, UFOs, etc — was able to pick up and activate. Or maybe my own spirit helpers were able to receive the broadcasted mental request for help and were able to go immediately to the aid of the ailing rabbit. Or, again, Pat's release from tension and worry over the rabbit, when she found a possible solution, allowed her own healing power to flow. Or perhaps her own guides, spirit helpers, sub-conscious or Higher Self, worked through her physical body to bring about the cure.'

Marilyn Preston believes that 'our minds are literally broadcasting stations all the time'. She believes too that it is easier to send messages out than to receive them.

'Did you feel any depletion at the time mentioned by Mrs Forster?' I asked. Pat Forster is certain the date was 2 August 1975 and that the time was one p.m.

'I had badly scalded my hand the first day of August,' Marilyn Preston recalled, 'and on 2 August the main thing I was aware of was this terribly painful hand, frustration at not being able to do any typing and a wonderment as to why my hand had suffered this ''accident''.

'From day to day I go up and down mentally and spiritually . . . it could be that people are ''tuning in'' to me . . . if a friend or patient feels depressed, I've often found myself in very low spirits at the same time . . . and have only discovered it later, when I've received

11. Waterfall at St Nectan's Glen: 'Many are the stories . . .
chanting of monks at night; invisible sobbing . . .'

12.   Jeannette on the subject of luck: 'Happy and excited on the inside and yet you're contented at the same time . . . it's a strange mixture.'

13. Gypsy Smith — Jeannette's Aunt.

14. Hawker's Hut, Morwenstow: 'Some people are quite convinced that Robert Stephen Hawker still haunts his Cornish parish.'

15. Morwenstow Church: 'A very haunted atmosphere . . .
take a look at the four graves of drowned sailors.'

16. & 17.   The Bush Inn, Morwenstow: 'Several people claimed to have had unusual experiences here.'

18.   Morwenstow Cliffs: '. . . this cliffscape wears a storm well.'

19.   Fay Glossop: 'You can tell the kind of person you're dealing with by his or her aura.'

their letter, asking for help.'

Marilyn Preston quotes Dr Arthur Guirdham, a well-known re-incarnationist and author: 'Some people are "receptors". They are receptive to the actual suffering of others. And I know this to be true. For instance, last Thursday I had the most terrible backache which made me feel sick and in constant pain . . . Yet I felt it was not *my* pain. Then on Saturday I had a message from a friend needing urgent healing who had been in agony from a slipped disc since *Thursday morning*. I gave him healing on Saturday evening. The healing took away the sharpness of my own pain, and the man patient was able to get around much easier.'

Further testimony of Marilyn Preston's healing power at long range came to me from Anne Smail of Burgess Hill in Sussex.

'When our miniature beagle, Simon, now fourteen years old, was ten years old, he tore a ligament badly in his left back leg. The vet did all he could to no avail. When Simon was ten and a half years old and practically unable to walk on that leg, the hip of which was wasting away, the vet said that the only hope now — and that a slim one — was for him to cut into the knee joint and pack it with cortisone,' Anne Smail told me.

'One Thursday I wrote to Marilyn telling her that we were terribly worried about an anaesthetic for Simon at his age and asking her, if we had the operation done, whether she could help Simon recover. The following Sunday my husband took Simon for his daily painful walk, but returned soon after looking utterly amazed. He said, "I don't know what has happened but Simon is not limping," and there was Simon standing firmly on four legs. He has not limped since. On the Monday morning we had a letter from Marilyn. She said that on the Saturday she had given Simon his operation, mentally — from Saltash!

'A few months later Simon had a sore eye so we took him to the same vet for ointment. He was extremely surprised that Simon was the "dog with the leg" and could find nothing wrong with it. We told him what Marilyn had done and he said, "Quite right too, more and more vets and doctors are turning to healers for that extra something we cannot give".'

Marilyn Preston, for her part, is convinced absent healing can cover any kind of distance. She once had an appeal for help from as far away as Australia. Moreover she believes that, despite the thousands of miles separating her and the patient, the healing still

worked. 'Now isn't that a fine advertisement for absent healing . . .
all the way to the other side of the world?'

Another animal experience brought me back to Tintagel.

The Castle may be only a ruin, but it remains an awe-inspiring
sight in spite of missing masonry.

Below the castle ruins lies Tintagel beach, tiny and disappointing
with pebbles of rounded slate, a poor substitute for the golden sands
of nearby Bossiney or Trebarwith Strand. Close by is a diminutive
waterfall. Something that will certainly not disappoint is Merlin's
Cave where legend says the wizard discovered the infant Arthur
washed ashore. Lying directly below the ruins, the cave pierces the
great cliff, leading to a miniature rocky beach on the other side.

Arthur, of course, has grown into a big bone of contention. His-
torians have been arguing for years. Did he reign in reality or
fantasy? Was it at Tintagel or somewhere else?

However our visit to Tintagel beach, one grey wintery morning,
had nothing to do with King Arthur. Or did it? Our destination was
Merlin's Cave. And 'we' meant Spiritualists Alan Nance and Fay
Glossop, plus an anonymous local Spiritualist, Rex, our Welsh collie
cross, photographer Paul Broadhurst and myself.

Fay, who in the opinion of Alan Nance, is good at detecting
atmospheres, admitted: 'I felt a tremendous pressure on my head,
and my heart started racing as I entered the cave. There's something
there. Had I been alone I would probably have picked up more. The
atmosphere of Merlin's Cave could definitely affect some people,
and this could trigger fear. But personally I felt nothing sinister.
There's something rather special about this whole Tintagel area. The
very first time I went to Tintagel, I felt worried and wanted to get
away from the place. As far as Merlin's Cave was concerned today, I
felt drawn to one spot in particular . . . I felt more power there than
anywhere else in the cave. However, there was nothing evil. I would
have sensed that before I had even gone into the cave.'

Alan Nance, for his part, thought conditions were against psychic
investigation. 'People walking to and fro were not helpful. On a
quieter day, and given a longer period of time, deeper concentration
would almost certainly have produced more reaction. You need time
and no outside influences to build up the right condition.'

The reason for our appearance here was a letter written to me by Irene Ionides of Woolmer Lodge, Liss Forest in Hampshire. More than fifteen years earlier, Miss Ionides, then resident in Cornwall, took her dog Panda, a Dalmation cross bitch, into this same Merlin's Cave.

'Half way through the cave,' wrote Irene Ionides, 'she stopped and shivered and started screaming. When Panda started cowering and screaming, I suddenly felt the hairs on my neck rise and my one idea was to pull her back and get her out into the open air again. So I turned back and we ran shorewards again and she quickly quietened down. A man standing near the cave said: ''I know exactly how your dog feels . . . I can feel something sinister in this spot!'' I had to agree with him . . . there *was* some evil influence there. I am responsive to atmosphere, but never to that extent. As for Panda, she was used to Cornish coves and beaches. Moreover she never behaved in that manner either before or after that day . . . and I've never been back.'

But on this Sunday morning, our Welsh collie cross experienced no such fear. He showed a good deal of caution on entering the cave, but within five minutes or even less had satisfied himself there was nothing to worry about.

However, neither Alan Nance nor Fay Glossop discounted Miss Ionide's claim. 'Something was certainly there at the time of the incident . . . and the behaviour of the dog proves this, for all animals are psychic.'

For me, at least, one question had been answered.

5
Auras

Fay Glossop at St Austell

'What are auras?' I asked Fay Glossop.

'It's the colour surrounding a person or an animal or an object. It's rather like a rainbow. If you're psychic, you can see this light, but it's not a constant, consistent light. The shades vary according to the moods of the person. Actually there are two auras: the etheric aura, which is close to the body, and deeper in shade . . . and the astral aura . . . that's much finer, not so dense. It's very delicate, and I've only seen it twice. This shows everything about the person.

Disease shows itself in the aura *before* making itself felt in the body. It's shown up by variations in the main colour or by the fading out of colour. The aura's the blueprint of our lives from birth to death and records our mental, spiritual and emotional levels. Given long enough experience and research into the subject of auras, it's even possible to reveal the characteristics of parents and grand-parents. It may though take hours to build up with an ever widening aura of several feet in width which contains the details.

'Each conscious state has its own wavelength and colour. The magnetic or auric sensitivity accounts for many of our changes of feeling and responses to conditions outside ourselves . . . yet it also has a bearing on our inward natures. In illness or extreme fear the aura contracts close to the body, as if to protect . . . while in harmonious conditions it extends.'

Fay, a ladies' hairstylist, living and working in St Austell in the heart of the China Clay country, has qualified as a healer through the National Federation of Spiritual healers. 'It was only when I started healing that I started seeing auras.' She was born in Falmouth, spent her childhood in Cornwall and then moved to Wales. 'I came back to Cornwall in 1963 . . . really there's no place quite like Cornwall, and I don't think I could ever leave it again.'

She did, however, have one confession. 'The trouble is no two mediums seem to agree about this subject. Different people have different interpretations.'

'Do colours then have a certain significance?'

'Oh, yes, very much so. Clear blue is a very spiritual colour. Pink is for compassion. Green, I see as a healing colour.

'Most mediums though are agreed on one thing: they don't like to see red. Red isn't considered a very spiritual colour. It's usually the aura of a very earthy person. Though again it depends on the shade of red. Scarlet, for example, can mean energy and vitality.

'The aura usually surrounds the head and shoulders. The more you study it, the clearer it becomes, but you can concentrate too hard, and fail to see it. The more relaxed, usually the better the aura. That's my experience anyway.

'We all wear a mask, sometimes more than one mask. But seeing the aura helps you to see the real personality. Our aura, you could say, is the garment we'll take with us when we leave this place and go into the spirit world.'

'How do you tune in for getting an aura sighting?'

'It's a kind of daydreaming really. A sort of looking into the distance.

'You can tell the kind of person you're dealing with by his or her aura. Yours for the moment is mauve . . .'

'Is that good or bad?'

She smiled broadly. 'That's good . . . it shows a spiritual quality. A mixture of the pink for compasssion and the blue standing for a spiritual something. Whenever I see blue or one of the delicate shades in the aura, I say to myself: "You can talk to this person about spiritual matters . . . they won't try and ridicule you. They'll be sympathetic and understanding."

'Yes, the aura is a kind of identi-kit of the inner personality. I remember seeing a narrow, very narrow band around the head of somebody, and I instinctively thought "Trouble here!" and I was dead right. He turned out to be one of the meanest men I've ever met! When the aura tends to be dark and murky, you can be practically certain that you're dealing with a very materialistic type of person . . . as events proved with the man I've just mentioned.'

'What about patients who come to you for spiritual healing? Does the aura help you?'

She looked thoughtful for a few moments. 'Yes, you could say that the aura is a form of diagnosis. Diagnosis in healing, though, can be strange. Somebody came to me recently, and I picked up a chest condition . . . now this person wasn't suffering from a chest complaint, but her neighbour was! You might have a woman in for healing, and detect the health trouble of her husband. The diagnosis can somehow be indirect, and related to another person close to the patient.

'You can usually tell the *very* ill patient by the aura. A dull red usually tells me that the person is suffering from some form of cancer. Green and blue I usually associate with nervous disorders.'

'What about black?'

'I've never seen black . . . and never want to, for that would be a very evil person!'

'How about animals?' I asked. 'Does the aura differ greatly from that surrounding human beings?'

'No,' Fay explained, 'as we have different personalities, so have animals. If the mood of a person changes, so does his or her aura. And the same applies to dogs, cats, horses, all animals in fact, their auras vary according to their personalities. Watching birds in flight can be quite fascinating because there you get the different colours moving.'

'And what about death? When a person dies . . . what happens to the aura then?'

'In death, the aura fades, it lingers for about an hour, getting fainter and fainter, and then finally vanishing. I've never been present when a person has died, but I did see one patient very close to death . . . within a day of passing on . . . and the aura became a greeny yellow, a very murky yellow. It had lost all its old lustre and I was certain death was not far away.'

Since that conversation with Fay Glossop, I have seen illustrations by Kirlian photography, claiming to show this unseen force — the aura — in the now extinct *Fate and Fortune:* the fingertip of a healthy human being showing flares of luminous gas around the physical body and, in contrast, a leaf dying through lack of nutrition with a blood red stain covering the entire surface.

The same *Fate and Fortune* article claimed: 'Mediums and spiritualists, who have seen Kirlian photographs, have from the start said they are physical representations of the aura. They share the same major characteristics — both are colourful, changing displays around the physical body; both are radically affected by altered mood or health; both react sensitively to the presence of others.

'The Kirlian photographs of faith healers, which have been the subject of experiments in the USA, are especially interesting. In their quiet, non-healing state, the healers' fingertips show normal blue displays. But when they are at work the displays grow much more intense, brighten to orange and white, and spread out to sheets of colour rather than flares.'

There was also a photograph of a scorpion, showing 'the vivid and unmistakable light pattern of a living organism.' I was interested also in two photographs of a geranium leaf: the first of the leaf in a healthy state with 'the typical blue flare structure around the tips,' and the second revealing colour changes on its surface after it had been deprived of light for seventy-two hours.

I asked Fay whether she thought these shots were really of auras — or some clever trick photography.

'They're different from the auras I see,' she admitted. 'Those I see are pulsating; they're constantly changing their colours . . . one shade blending with another. But even so I think these photos are genuine because they take on the same patterns as those I see.'

She looked pensive again.

'The more spiritual a person, the more compassionate their nature, the easier it is to see their aura.'

6
Healing

Barney Camfield at Plymouth

That perceptive author, Ronald Duncan, once reflected: 'To move from one house to another is to do more than change one's address. We think it is merely a matter of shifting our furniture, buying new curtains, finding new tradesmen . . . and assume quite confidently that our personality will soon impose itself on our new surroundings . . . That is where we make a big mistake: it is not we who change a house but, more often, the house which changes us.'

Another Westcountry man who took this theme a stage further, when I was researching for *Supernatural in Cornwall*, was the Reverend Frederick William Marshall, then Vicar of Cury and Gunwalloe. 'I go down to Gunwalloe almost every day,' he explained, 'and very often I am conscious of something deeply spiritual there. I've never seen anything, but I've many times felt surrounded by the departed. At service, when I say ''The Lord be with thy spirit'', I get a response that goes beyond the number of those present. The odour of past prayer hangs about the place.'

Almost immediately on entering the high-ceilinged drawing-room of Barney Camfield's home, I remembered both men, for this room is filled with a wonderful peace and sense of harmony, due surely to the healing work that goes on here. Outside it was a wet Plymouth with pavements shining from torrential rain, but in this room there was - in spirit - a golden glow.

Healing had brought me back over the Tamar into Devon — one healer in particular.

Barney Camfield lives at 53 Amherst Road in Pennycomequick, Plymouth. He is Chairman of the Plymouth Healing Fellowship, which is a non-profit-making charitable organization, and a Unitarian Minister.

Bespectacled, bearded and in a brown suit, you might think Barney Camfield was a media man rather than a healer — and your thinking wouldn't be wrong either. He had only a few months before retired early from Westward Television where he worked on the sales side and in public relations. Earlier in his career he was involved with film production and before that he'd done some farming. He has the air of a media man in that he can hold an audience. A friend, who had heard him speak at a public meeting, told me 'he's very theatrical,' and yet here in his clinic with patients or helpers, he had that ability to remain patiently quiet, consciously or unconsciously making them feel perfectly at ease, allowing them to be the centre of attention.

What is healing?

Some people wrap the whole thing in an aura of mystery. But Barney Camfield is not one of them. 'Healing,' he said, 'sometimes prefixed with the words "Spiritual", "Faith", "Divine" or "Natural", is looked upon by some as mysterious, by others perhaps as a "con". "Faith" — meaning either a belief that healing will be effective or a belief in a power such as God — is not necessary. Healing works without such beliefs as many can attest - to their surprise! "Spiritual" or "Divine" it may be but such a claim is not easy to prove. "Yahweh", the Hebrew for that which we call God, is a word which is related to the Hebrew verb "to be" and means "to be actively present". This we may understand to be true but find it difficult to demonstrate to others.

'Modern science, however, says that there is "energy" present everywhere and that even the most solid material object — including the human body — is composed of atoms which are themselves composed of energy. This energy is certainly then "natural" and is above us, below us and in and through us all. It is actively present and in it we live, move and have our being.

'What does happen in "Healing" is that energy is transferred from the healer to the patient; usually via the hands which are placed on or near the patient. This transfer of energy can usually — but not always — be felt by the patient as heat, cold, tingling or as sensations which can be experienced but cannot be described.

'This energy from healers has been recorded with scientific electronic equipment. The flow of ultra-violet from the hands, for example, has been found to increase by up to a thousand times if it is needed by the patient. Other subtle energies are transmitted and atomic structural changes have been scientifically observed after the "laying on of hands".

'Patients usually experience a gradual betterment with successive treatments of varying lengths of time. Sometimes rapid, sometimes slow. And sometimes there is an increase of pain for a time which can be felt — in some arthritic patients, for example — up to twenty-four hours after treatment. An indication it seems of physical, structural re-adjustment.

'Again, many scientific tests have been made which indicate that "healing" cannot harm but does bring the body — and the mental and emotional states — to a harmonious balance.'

Barney Camfield has a recipe, too, for success. In a paper, first published in 1955, entitled *Do you know what you want?*, he explained his philosophy as follows: 'First of all you will find that it is completely useless to attempt to succeed at anything at all if you consciously allow thoughts of failure or the sense of depression to remain in your mind. Think of something positive and cheerful — BE OPTIMISTIC! — and you will cancel the wrong thoughts out.

'Secondly: don't try too hard for success; just confidently hope and expect it to arrive. If you try and force things you are liable to make mistakes and be clumsy over it. The same law is in force, you see; if you *believe* that the job in hand is hard, then your subconscious will see that you do the wrong things, in order to make it hard! You can safely leave it to your subconscious mind to prompt you and give you ideas. You will know when to make a move and when to sit tight and do nothing.

'Thirdly: keep on thinking of yourself as you wish to be - completely ignoring the failures you have had in the past.

'Fourthly: make sure of your goal before you allow your subconscious to guide you on your way. Ask yourself quite honestly what it is you want — *and why you want it!* Do you want to be wealthy? Why? Because being wealthy you think that you will then be happy? Do you want to be famous — as a musician or an athlete? Why? — Because it'll make you happy? That's the real goal — HAPPINESS! That's what you are really after!'

I asked Barney Camfield how he began his healing.

'It was nearly thirty years ago when I was living in West Cornwall. I went into a chemist and one of the girls serving in the shop said she was suffering with a very bad headache and, looking absolutely grey, she sat down on a chair . . . in those days they had chairs in shops . . . and I simply placed my hand on her head and tried to say a few soothing words. And after a few minutes she said, "It's gone! It's gone!'' and it all began from there.' He admits that in his early days as a healer there was a good deal of anti attitudes by doctors and hospitals, but that he says has almost completely vanished — to such an extent that he is a welcome visitor to many Plymouth hospitals.

We then talked about success and failure.

'Several hundred patients come to us during the course of the year and I would say that as many as eighty per cent are either cured or helped and even with the remaining twenty per cent I would hesitate to use the word failure as we — through healing — enable patients to face the end of their earthly life with a different frame of mind. To put it bluntly somebody may have incurable cancer and healing helps them to die more easily . . . who is to say that is failure?'

Certainly on my visit to 53 Amherst Road I saw two patients go out of the house seemingly different people from those who had come in. One, an elderly bent grey-haired lady, suffering from Parkinson's Disease, following healing, went out of the room with decidedly better movements.

The other patient, a man, I'd noted when he'd come into the room. He had a grey, apprehensive look. Half-an-hour later, after healing, he was wearing a more relaxed, more assured expression — looking a completely changed person. 'This is only my third visit to the clinic,' he told me, 'but in little more than a week I've cut my drug intake by half . . . and I'm feeling so much better . . .' His was a very sad story: acute depression, loss of job, break-up of marriage. 'I don't blame my wife for leaving me . . . I was a pretty hopeless case.' When he left the house, an hour later, I felt he was no longer that. Barney Camfield and his helpers had clearly given him new hope. They'd set him on the right road. You could tell it: the way he walked.

The clinic's methods of healing include Reflexology which is healing by the manipulation of the patient's feet. 'There's nothing new about this,' he says 'the ancient Egyptians and the Chinese and Japanese were doing it centuries ago, as were the Indians in the new world.'

Barney Camfield and his helpers are convinced that if we gave just a few minutes each day to massaging our feet many health problems could be averted. 'The soles of most people's feet are tough especially around the heel,' he says, 'so the massage must be deep and pressure very firm if the reflexes are to be reached, and if you encounter pain, that means a congested area has been found.' He likened this to a blocked sink where water trickles away and a plunger is used to remove the obstruction, allowing the water to flow freely. 'In the same way when pain is experienced in the foot or around the ankle that represents a blocked or congested area, and by working systematically over the area, the extra stimulation will often disperse the blockage. Much, though, depends on how seriously ill the patient is.'

A complete massage takes about fifteen minutes, and when any part of the foot is painful to the healer's touch, then something is wrong. According to Reflexology our feet are a kind of map of our physical condition. The head, for example, corresponds to the toes; the spine to the bones along the inside of the foot, stretching from heel bone to the base of the big toe — if that area is sore to the touch this means there is trouble in the spinal column. I can speak from some personal experience as on my first visit massage of my toes brought immediate relief to a sinus condition that had been plaguing me for some months.

The clinic also uses hypnosis in certain cases. 'Hypnotic power lies in the *acceptance* of the idea suggested,' Barney Camfield explained. 'For example, in the induction process suggestions that the room is getting warmer and that the subject is getting more sleepy can be made. If these ideas are not accepted — believed — then sleep will not follow. If they are accepted then the subject can fall asleep; when his judgement — his ability to evaluate — has stopped functioning.'

But he has not used deep hypnosis for twenty-five years, preferring patients or students, while sleepy or fully relaxed, to be aware of all that is being said. 'They are still capable of rejecting any suggestion and returning to full consciousness whenever they wish.'

In full flow, when making a point, the words come from him with the fluency of a man who occupies the Unitarian pulpit at Mortonhampstead every Sunday, and he can add the occasional dramatic gesture that rightly earns that word 'theatrical'. Yet the same person who called him 'theatrical' later saw him giving a public demonstration of regression under light hypnosis and commented on 'his quiet approach and his low profile throughout'.

In private conversation, he has a marvellous sense of timing. Sonia and I joined him and his wife and two colleagues for a delicious vegetarian lunch. It was a delightful experience in that he uncannily knows when to come into the conversation almost as if he senses when the other person has come to their final assessment or observation. His conversation has a clairvoyant quality. There are no awkward silences either, for he has the ability to lead the talk up some related but new and exciting avenue. In his company, whether operating as a healer or merely enjoying conversation over food and drink — he's a teetotaller and a vegetarian whenever possible — you find Life is suddenly more purposeful. He talks about remarkable happenings as some people might talk about a TV programme they saw last night or the news on this morning's radio. 'I avoid the word "miracle" like the plague as I think all things work according to "natural" laws; some of which, however, are not perhaps generally known.' Above all, he has the ability to instil confidence — that at least was my impression. Sonia and I agreed he must be a tremendous morale-booster as a hospital visitor. His very handshake, on first meeting, is reassuring — the sure sign of healing hands perhaps.

Certainly when he lays hands on you for healing, you are aware of an immediate power and warmth. That anyway was my experience for I felt an injection of fresh energy. Though I had received healing on previous occasions from other very gifted healers, I had never quite experienced such a heightened sense of well-being for such a period of time. It was on a Friday morning that Barney Camfield laid his hands on my shoulders and back, while Anne Stephens, a qualified masseuse and reflexologist, worked her reflexology technique on my toes, and I can honestly say that I was conscious of this inflow of new energy for more than forty-eight hours.

Apart from all this, I found his body language particularly fascinating. He explained how our physical frailties often reveal our thinking and very attitude to Life.

'I know of a number of deaf people who have been, to say the least, disinclined to listen to other people's points of view where it meant relinquishing cherished ideas. Dr Crookshank once said that there is more than coincidence in the truth that those who totter in shoes too small for them — and on high heels — are cramped in their "understanding".

'The man who has a raging headache is repressing something about which he would really like to rage. A wheezing patient has something which he should get off his chest. We could tell him to "cough it up".

'Dr Crookshank even suggested that we could well look into the psychological problems of those suffering from diarrhoea and constipation. I agree. There was an expression, common when I was in the Forces, which referred to the fact that fear can loosen the bowels! I think that the symbolic meaning behind this is that the person afflicted feels that he is losing his hold! Likewise a constipated individual may have the fear of losing something but is desperately holding on.

'I have found that those who are worried about responsibility tend to develop pains in their shoulders. Do we not speak of "shouldering" responsibility? In a number of cases, too I have been concerned with people whose shoulder troubles lead me to think that it depends upon their emotional response as to which shoulder is affected. For example, if the individual is shouldering some responsibility which he does not want but cannot get rid of then the left shoulder is affected. If, on the other hand, there is some responsibility which he wishes to assume but cannot do so, then the right shoulder is affected.

'This is so, too, with the legs. These appear to be affected in a symbolic manner with "progress" of one sort or another; it may be physical progress from one place to another or progress in marriage, studies or in career. If the individual feels that he is making progress in the wrong direction — which includes lack of progress on some course — and his attention and consequent emotional stress is focussed upon this progress in the wrong direction - then the left leg will be affected. If his attention is upon progress he would like to make but cannot, then his right leg would be affected. In other words, two men could both be making little progress in their jobs. One with his attention and frustration focussed upon his present position could, through unconscious emotional stress, express the frustration physically, in the left leg. His co-worker in a similar state of lack of progress but with his, perhaps largely unconscious, mental attention on the goal he has set, would express his emotional tension through some physical disorder in the right leg.

'The actual site of physical trouble in the body need not, perhaps, be deeply hidden symbolically. Whilst it is possible that, say, cancer of the breast is symbolic of a frustration of some kind being "harboured" in a woman's breast, it is extremely likely that it is a result of an energy frustration connected with motherhood. Symbolic yes, but not exactly hidden.

'The expression, "He caught a cold over that", meaning a disappointing setback, perhaps, to a business deal, refers to the background disappointment. Why ''caught a cold''? In my experience colds are associated with being sorry for oneself which could certainly apply in connection with a setback or being bested in a business deal.

'We use these expressions carelessly   they are, perhaps, something on a par with ''old wives tales'' — but it seems to me that, in the past, some observant people did realise the connections between emotions and their physical affects. We seem to have forgotten that there is a reason behind some of those old sayings which we use simply as figures of speech.'

Normally Barney Camfield and his helpers operate clinics five days a week at 53 Amherst Road — Monday to Friday — an appointment is always appreciated, either by letter or telephone. Apart from these, there are 'open' clinics at the Unitarian Church in Notte Street, Plymouth, on Saturdays, and one in his Unitarian Church at Mortonhampstead on Sundays. Barney Camfield also does herbal prescriptions and the clinic is able to help patients with absent healing.

'We get people from all over the place,' he told me. 'Only this week I had a patient who had come down from Bristol, and last week there was someone who had made the journey especially from Wales. If a patient cannot get to us, we try to give them the name and address of a reputable healer in their area. Alternatively we can give them absent or distant healing. This, we think, may operate through healing thought working in telepathic co-operation with the ''field of energy''.'

When I left Plymouth that Friday I felt absent healing could work for *some* people, and Barney Camfield must have sensed reservations, for some time after he telephoned me and asked how my sinus was. The blocking unfortunately had returned; yet within minutes of his talking on the phone I felt freer and altogether more relaxed. He stressed that he was not employing hypnosis, and I was totally convinced that absent healing *works*.

Nevertheless those patients, who meet him face-to-face, are lucky people.

7
Some Cornish Hauntings

Cornwall — or parts of her — have a haunted and haunting quality. She probably has more haunted acreage than any other part of Britain. We, Cornish, may not readily admit it, but most of us treat these matters seriously.

At very least, we are superstitious. I wonder, for instance, how many St Levan parents, down in West Cornwall, would christen a baby daughter Joanna, knowing there is an old Penwith tradition that any child christened that name at Parchapel Well is destined to be ill-wished or a fool.

So, in this Occult exploration, across the Westcountry, I decided to do a tour of some Cornish hauntings, starting at Morwenstow in North Cornwall. In fact Morwenstow is no bad place to begin any tour of Cornwall. The wind whistles in from the Atlantic only four furlongs away. Roughly halfway between Bude and Hartland, there is no village: a church, a vicarage, an inn, an aged farm, now partly shop and partly tea room, offering accommodation. It is contrasting country: deep, wooded combe and towering jagged cliffs; ablaze with flowers in season, then robbed of colour; invaded by visitors in summer, deserted in winter. It's a last corner of Cornwall before Welcombe and England begins. 'Here,' reflected Sir John Betjeman, 'one is reaching not only the end of Cornwall, but it seems the end of the world.'

There is — for me — a very haunted atmosphere about Morwenstow. Take a look at the four graves of drowned sailors in the churchyard and then go out onto those Morwenstow cliffs, preferably on a stormy day for this cliffscape wears a storm well, and you'll understand why the famous Parson Hawker wrote:

> *From Hartland Point to Padstow Light*
> *Is a watery grave by day and by night.*

20. Cornish cliffs near Land's End: 'The bones of this land
are not speechless.'

21.   Barney Camfield and Anne Stephens at work on a patient.

22. Barney Camfield: 'This energy from healers has been recorded with scientific electronic equipment.'

23. & 24.   Dozmary Pool: 'In certain lights Dozmary
sparkles like a jewel, but at times a heavy
melancholy hangs.'

25. & 26.   Golitha Falls near Draynes Bridge on River
Fowey: 'Take a look at the map of the Moor . . .
the very names quicken the imagination . . . such
places read like extracts of a novel.'

27. Charlotte Miller — psychic painter: 'I don't hear an actual voice, instructing me to paint. But I have come to recognise the time.'

28. Carole Eager: 'He had died of a heart attack . . . no
more a dream, but a living nightmare.'

29.   Brown Willy seen from Rough Tor: 'The moor is Supernatural territory . . .'

On the subject of the Supernatural, Robert Stephen Hawker had a habit of changing his stance. In one mood he was capable of a hoax; in another he would seriously affirm. On one occasion, as a young man, he pretended to be a ghost and he did a good job of it, hoodwinking local folk into believing that a mermaid sat on the rocks in silvery moonlight. For several nights the mermaid appeared, flashing her mirror and singing strange songs, while the number of inquisitive people multiplied. Hawker however tired of sitting in the cold, clad only in seaweed — and the mermaid never appeared again.

Later in his Ministry, though, he claimed Supernatural experience to the extent of *seeing* Saint Morwenna, and, over the years, he became convinced in the power of the Evil Eye, once attributing to a witch's curse the fact that he lost nine sucking-pigs. 'The sow which, like Medea, had taken a hatred to her own offspring, spurning them away from her milk . . . the evil eye of old Cherry (the witch) had turned the mother's heart to stone, and she let them die one by one . . .'

During Hawker's ministry a violent thunderstorm passed over the parish, uprooting trees, killing cattle and setting ricks on fire, and, once more, some of the superstitious blamed old Cherry for the disasters.

A fire, in fact, was one of the reasons that had brought me to Morwenstow. The Bush Inn for many years had boasted a fine thatched roof, but in November 1968 a fire destroyed this lovely old roof and roughly half this ancient inn. The Bush, happily, has long resumed business but sadly minus its thatch — though inside it generates a genuine old-world atmosphere.

Jim Gregory, the proprietor, told me the story of the fire and how some people claimed to have seen a dark shadowy figure moving away from the blazing building. 'I was assured it wasn't a billow of smoke, it had too much substance for that . . . I'm not saying it was a spirit or a ghost but the interesting thing is that we had had lots of strange happenings up to the date of the fire . . . and it seemed that the fire had killed them off — or almost. Several people claimed to have had unusual experiences here, and we, ourselves, had heard footsteps upstairs and on the staircase when we *knew* there was no one about who could possibly make such noises. We had, over the years, a real floor show of noises, for which there was no rational explanation. And for a time we thought the fire had really removed this spirit, but then about six years ago an American lady was staying here and one afternoon she went to her room and discovered this elderly seafaring character there, someone dressed in old-fashioned clothes. ''What are you doing here?'' she asked. But without replying, he turned and simply vanished through the wall!

'Then we had a clergyman friend of the family who often came to stay with us. We put him into what we considered the best room in the inn but, to our surprise, he asked to be moved to another room. ''I feel menaced at night,'' he explained, ''I can't sleep in that room.'' He saw a shape and felt its presence leaning over the bed.'

Jim Gregory is reluctant to overtell the unusual events in the years since the fire. 'At first we thought the fire had killed it off completely, but it hasn't exactly done that. At least it has reduced the number of unusual incidents.' Some cynics believe that hoteliers and innkeepers deliberately invent stories of ghosts to attract customers. That may be so, but Jim Gregory convinced me of his sincerity.

Though nobody has succeeded in identifying the ghost of the Bush, some people are quite convinced that Robert Stephen Hawker still haunts his Cornish parish. Mrs Constance Drummond of Stratton told me of an occurrence between the two wars. 'One evening a friend and I were walking back from Morwenstow with my retriever dog. We *both* heard footsteps behind us. There was a corner, and we both paused. I said: ''Oh, let's wait for whoever it is to pass.'' We stopped, and noticed that my dog had flattened himself into the hedge. The footsteps came on round the corner, passed us, and went on. No one to be seen. At a cottage higher up, I asked a woman if the lane was haunted. ''Oh, yes,'' she said brightly, ''Parson Hawker often comes up after being at the church . . .'''

Someone else who agrees Cornwall is a haunted landscape is Cornish author Joan Rendell who lives near Launceston. Moreover she speaks from first-hand experience.

'I remember driving back from St Austell one evening with a local bank manager; we'd been attending a meeting down there and it was nearly twilight. We were on the A30 crossing Bodmin Moor, on the Bodmin side of Bolventor near the Hawk's Tor pit, when I saw this beautiful stone circle on the left-hand side of the road. My companion saw it, too, and we both remarked how beautiful the stones were, and I resolved to take a closer look at them when I next came that way. I intended taking photographs but when I came to the spot on my next visit I couldn't find them. They simply weren't there . . . they'd vanished! And we both had been perfectly sober . . . I've drunk nothing but water all my life. I've travelled that road many times since, but I've never seen anything resembling that stone circle.'

Later Joan Rendell showed me a tree-flanked lane, leading to a farmhouse not far from her home. 'That's a haunted house,' she said, 'and this is a haunted lane.' And as she related a whole string of strange incidents, I was convinced she spoke the truth. 'I was engaged to a young man in the Navy during the war, and he stayed there. I remember how he came over to us, one morning, saying that he'd been kept awake during the night by a horse clattering around the farmyard, and yet the farmer had assured him there was no horse on the farm. Later we learned from Conan Doyle that poltergeists often manifest themselves as horses, creating the sound of hooves.

'There was a dog too at the farm, an aged dark-coloured collie cross who came over to our home every day, and I took him back to the farm every evening, and put him in a barn where he would sleep. You went up about fifteen feet to the door of that barn. Well, one night about half past three there was this terrible scratching and scraping on our back door. It was the farm dog. Next morning the farmer came round and asked ''Have you seen the dog?'' He then told us how, during the night, the dog had bitten away the bottom half of the door to get out of the barn, and had leapt fifteen feet to get away — astonishing really for the dog was then fourteen years old. Something must have terrified him because he never went back to the farm. He spent the rest of his life with us. Several times I tried to walk him back, but he'd get so far up that lane and that was it . . . he wouldn't go beyond the last tree.'

Joan Rendell had had strange, inexplicable experiences inside the farmhouse itself.

'A man hanged himself around the turn of the century in the kitchen from one of those hooks they used for hanging hams. Well, it was a Christmas, shortly after my father's death in 1953, and mother and I were invited over to the farm for our Christmas dinner. During the meal mother said ''Stop shaking my chair!'' But I said, ''Why I'm not doing anything to your chair, mother!'' And then as if to prove to me that my mother was quite right, my chair started shaking too . . . and it went on shaking for the rest of the meal. When the meal was finished, we left promptly but politely. That was one Christmas dinner I didn't enjoy!

'My family have known that house for a good many years, and it's never been a very lucky place. In the days when it was part of the farm, people in it were usually in poor health, and the land surrounding it didn't do well, and livestock tended to die. Somebody said, ''That place has been cursed!'' Maybe they were correct.

'Before we had a telephone here I often did telephoning from that farmhouse rather than going up the road to the phone box, and I well remember, one Sunday evening, I had arranged to make an important business call, and the family had very kindly left the key under the mat as they were out visiting friends. I got inside but never made the phone call . . . almost as soon as I got inside the house I could hear footsteps upstairs . . . I can still hear them . . . and the house was deserted.'

Though she has never seen a ghost, Joan Rendell has strong premonitions, one concerning a former farmer of this very property. 'Every morning I went over to the farm to get our milk, and on this particular morning I suddenly thought, ''Frank, I'm never going to see you again!'' When I got back home with the milk, mother said, ''Have you seen a ghost?'' I hadn't but I'd seen Frank dissolve and I *knew* I wouldn't see him again. Early next morning, his brother-in-law came across from the farm to tell us Frank had died during the night. He was only forty-nine, and hale and hearty . . . all completely unexpected.

'On another occasion, I was planning to go on a Continental coach tour and I normally look forward to my overseas trips with keen anticipation. This time, I didn't. I had a feeling that something awful was going to happen, and travelling through Norway, some miles from Oslo, I had this premonition of disaster. A little duck-blue car shot out of a side road, compelling our coach driver to swing off course, and the coach went over on its side. All was pandemonium and smashed glass. But I climbed out through the windscreen quite coolly as I'd seen it all happening just before . . . I'd even got hold of my camera case to protect it and had warned an Australian girl sitting beside me that an accident was coming . . . all just seconds before it happened.'

Inevitably after that stone circle story of Joan Rendell's on Bodmin Moor, I found myself heading for the Cornish wilderness. I looked, too, but in vain. However I used this stage of the journey as an excuse to revisit Dozmary Pool. A saucer-like depression to the south west of the Fowey Valley, it is a mile in circumference and 500 yards across. Sarah Foot, in her perceptive *Following the River Fowey*, said 'Its very beauty and surprising existence make it understandably a place to give birth to wondrous stories.' And though I have tended to steer clear of legends on this Occult journey, as I grow older I wonder whether there can be any smoke without fire, any *real* myth without *some* degree of reality. Dozmary and some of the remoter parts of the Moor provide landscapes that must surely make the cynics think again. Years ago a Spiritualist told me he found contact with the Spirit World easy on the rim of this lovely pool — in those days I knew next to nothing about the Supernatural and yet I didn't laugh as many young people might have done. For even then I knew Dozmary was no ordinary place. In certain lights Dozmary sparkles like a jewel, but at times a heavy melancholy hangs over this sheet of silent — or almost silent — water.

Maybe Sir Bedivere didn't throw Excalibur into Dozmary. Maybe Jan Tregeagle didn't vainly attempt to bail out Dozmary with a leaky limpet-shell. Maybe the Pool isn't bottomless. But you get the feeling that strange things could happen here, and possibly have.

I have sat in the saddle on Brown Willy, grateful tor a sturdy, sure-footed cob called Charlie and watched this world fade into a morning haze: a day when the wind slept and only birds and animals moved. On another morning I wedged myself between rocks on Rough Tor and attempted to hide from the invisible knife of the wind — and both times I was conscious of the same fact: the Moor *is* Supernatural territory.

Take a look at the map of the Moor: Twelve Men's Moor, Temple, where the Templars incredibly built a Norman church, in which couples were married without banns, Stripple Stones, Hawk's Tor, the Cheesewring, a colony of fantastic rocks — the very names quicken the imagination. Lord's Waste, Black Rock, Draynes, Maiden Tor and Hard Head, such places read like extracts from a novel.

I had the luck to know that very talented painter and author, Charles Simpson — even if only in the last years of his life. In his earlier days he had travelled over the Moor on his motorbike with paints and canvasses packed into a sidecar. It was he who helped me to understand the magic of Cornish moorland, particularly in that eerie period between sunset and darkness. 'The age at which history becomes obscure is typified by the hour of twilight when the hills loom huge above the sea and the tokens of man dead and man alive are swallowed up. As day departs, the power in the granite rouses itself to watch the approach of night. There wander abroad at such an hour many strange beings whose nature none can guess: emanations, influences, memories, shaping the little destinies which they enfold, some say for good, but more believe for ill — cloudy things that rove about the earth. They look through centuries and back beyond the sum of time through timeless ages, and hear the echoes of events in which their part is yet to be.'

To go from Bodmin Moor to the Lizard is to move from one Cornish world to another. The Lizard is the heel of Cornwall, the most southerly land in all Britain, and I was still on the Occult trail.

Cornwall has some lovely old buildings that have been turned into public houses, and my excursion of Cornish hauntings now took me beyond Helston, to the parish of Cury, to Bochym Manor. It was once called the Manor of Buchent, and early written records referred to a mulberry tree — which survives to this day. You can see it in the garden at the front of the house: indeed you are probably looking at one of the biggest and oldest mulberry trees in the country.

Bochym stands in a still green and sheltered valley: an idyllic setting; so much so that it's hard to believe its history has been so violent and bloody. A one-time owner was beheaded and the property was confiscated in the name of the Crown; while during the Civil War it became a Royalist stronghold, incurring the wrath of Cromwell, who destroyed the greater part of it. Then after the War it was rebuilt as a William and Mary mansion with a bowling green and terraced gardens. But tragedy struck again when Christopher Bellot had the harrowing experience of losing six daughters within the space of eight calendars, all victims of smallpox. After 1825, it was further extended by Stephen Davey, whose love of nature was such that he had plants brought to Bochym from many parts of the world. One hundred and fifty years on, many of those exotic plants are alive and well in this mild Lizard climate. Around the middle of the nine-

78

teenth century a secret path leading all the way to Mullion was discovered. With so many shadows in its history, it is inevitable that Bochym should have a haunted reputation. The darkest shadow of all was the murder of a young housemaid in 1708 whose body was found in the north attic. That section of the house was in the process of being renovated, but the work was never finished. To this day there are timbers shaped but not fitted, there is scaffolding and an unfinished wall, and if her ghost lurks, she would see very little change. The biggest change she would see is some electrical wiring which runs through this area of the house, and thereby hangs a story of fright.

Back in 1974, Stan May bought this property. 'I haven't seen any ghosts here,' he told me, 'but I well remember the day that the electricians were working here and one of them was in the attic. We had all sorts of people in the house working on various jobs. I remember the girl getting tea for the men at half past ten had worked out that we would require nineteen cups for nineteen workmen. But then she found she had one cup too many and thought she must have miscounted. ''No, you're right,'' somebody said, ''the electrician hasn't come down for his teabreak.'' Another person volunteered to give him a call in the attic; he went up and found this man cringing with fear. He was brought down for his tea, but never went back to finish the job. Even the foreman, in charge of the electricians, said he didn't feel happy up there, and they finished up doing the wiring with someone standing sentry at the door . . . they completed that part of the job very quickly.

'Also in 1974 when we were settling in here, my mother-in-law shared the same bedroom with my daughter Susan who was inclined to sleepwalk. My mother-in-law woke at about two o'clock in the morning and saw Susan standing at the window. She got up and went to guide Susan back when she realised that all the time Susan was fast asleep in her own bed. Not until after this did she know about a young nurse who had fallen out of that window.'

However, don't let these ghostly recollections deter you from visiting Bochym Manor. Once you pass the lodge gate you move into a little empire on its own, and inside the house you can be assured of a warm and friendly welcome from Stan May.

These are just a handful of Cornish hauntings, and in their different locations they prove that if you scratch the surface in Cornwall, in many places you will pick up echoes from the distant past.

8
Psychic Painting

Charlotte Miller at St Ives

Charlotte Miller's studio is the top of her home Crab Rock in the Warren, St Ives, with the sea only a pebble's throw from the window. Outside and beyond the windows is the vast, graceful sweep of St Ives Bay and, away in the distance, the white form of Godrevy Lighthouse.

St Ives, in some moods, is more akin to the Mediterranean and the Continent than Cornwall and the Atlantic, an impression intensified if there are Breton crabbers in the Bay.

It was the landscape painter J.M.W. Turner — a revolutionary in his own day but now generally acknowledged as the greatest British painter of all — who started the painting invasion of St Ives. He spent a winter here in 1818, revelling in the light and the exciting land and seascapes.

Today St Ives is the accepted art capital of Cornwall, and the artist — meaning the sculptor and the potter too — is an accepted member of local society. Times were, though, when he was viewed with suspicion. In the early days of the colony Louis Grier appeared on the wharf, on a *Sunday*, to do some painting, only to be told that if he and his easel dared show themselves again 'on the Lord's day', they would both end up in the harbour. There is also the lovely story of a fish cart being driven up steep Skidden Hill; the horse jibbing and the driver ending his string of abuse with the words 'You . . . you bloody artist!'

J. P. Hodin, writing in a Penwith Gallery brochure, paid tribute to the creative spirit of St Ives: 'Nowhere else in Europe, except in the South of France . . . have I found such creative energy as in the group of artists who have either lived permanently or temporarily in or around St Ives.'

Charlotte Miller has lived, for chapters of her life, in both Spain and Portugal, where she made friends with many artists. 1963 turned out to be a very significant year in her life and career as a painter: an introduction to Henrique Tavares of Lisbon, the Portuguese philosopher and poet, psychologist and painter. They became close companions and he was destined to have a strong influence on her painting and life style. She became his pupil for a special, and he claimed unique, style of abstract painting. 'Before meeting Henrique, I had concentrated on figurative painting,' she said, 'but he showed me his personal meaning of the word 'abstract' as applied to art. This, and a new insight inspired by his personal brand of philosophy, opened up new, exciting vistas in my life.'

Even today Charlotte Miller is reluctant to divulge the slightest hint about the method he has passed on to her. 'My paintings must speak for themselves. I don't even give them titles . . . my husband generally chooses titles for my work.

She believes that in some curious Supernatural way the colouring of her paintings are linked to the inner essence of the subject — and that the finished product reveals something of the soul of the subject.

By 1964 Charlotte Miller had become sufficiently proficient with her new technique to show her paintings in conjunction with Henrique Tavares — a two-man show at the Casa de Culture in Malaga.

As is sometimes the way with painters though, she largely neglected this side of her work for several years in favour of other ways and different ideas. Then she found her work, once more, veering back towards more figurative paintings. Recently though she became a member of a psychic circle in West Cornwall, and this Supernatural contact reawakened her interest in philosophical and psychic subjects — redirecting her painting energies along psychic lines.

'I have to be very quiet to do my psychic painting,' Charlotte Miller explained. 'I usually do it at night . . . I seem to do my best from about ten in the evening until midnight or even one or two o'clock. I don't hear any actual voice, instructing me to paint. But I have come to recognise the time, and with my psychic painting I work very fast indeed . . . an 8 by 8 that would take me hours in my conventional side, I can sometimes do in about 10 minutes flat. The other interesting thing is that whereas with say a seascape or a portrait I may spend hours finishing it, redoing this and that . . . highlighting some feature or adding something more . . . with psychic work I seem to know instinctively when it's finished. And once it's finished, there's never any need to go back and change anything.

'The important thing is that I mustn't be interrupted. If I'm interrupted, I become very bad tempered which is not my usual nature. Now, with my conventional painting I sit at an easel, but with my psychic painting I always stand and work on a flat surface . . . it's almost as if I have two painting personalities.'

Her work is certainly very different. Her conventional pictures owe something to Renoir and the Impressionists whom she greatly admires; whereas her psychic works are so different as if to suggest they have not been painted by the same person.

'How do you acount for the motivation of your psychic pictures?' I asked.

'I honestly don't know,' she said. 'But I have, for some time now, felt for quite certain that Henrique Tavares was dead. He always thought I had a lot of painting potential, but that I was not dedicated enough. I certainly feel as if a painter, from the past, is pushing me into these psychic moods. I'm not in a trance or anything like that but I definitely feel that I am being used as the painting instrument of someone or something.'

Charlotte Miller talks quietly. She has blue eyes, but not that piercing quality which so many psychic people possess. The impression is of a gentle person, and her three Jack Russell terriers reflect a deep love of animals as well as people.

Sometimes her paintings give hints as to the personality or the future of the person or persons who commissioned — or inspired — her work. And should the hints about the future appear too grim, Charlotte Miller confessed, 'I cannot bear to finish the painting. Luckily, it doesn't happen all that often. If it does, then I try and make some excuse, like saying I'm too busy to finish the painting. The burden of suspecting someone's future, especially if it looks bad, is awful.

'Some time ago, a newly married couple asked me to do some water colours for their new home. But when I came to paint them I found it so distressing that I never finished any of the paintings for that house. When I saw the girl a year later, she was terribly unhappy. She'd fallen in love with another man and the whole marriage was falling apart.'

There was another young couple who asked her to paint some pictures for themselves and their new baby. But once more the painter could not let them see her work. 'The paintings were grim and doom-laden, and one revealed a third adult figure, shadowy and among trees.' When Charlotte Miller next met the young woman, the significance of that third adult figure was explained. Bursting into tears, the young woman said she had fallen in love with a married man, whom she had met when walking in some woods.

An even more dramatic painting experience concerned an older woman client. 'I just could not get the painting to go at all . . . just ashes. A few days later the son of the woman phoned to say his mother had passed on.

'Another woman asked me to do a painting for herself and her husband, and though she had sent a photograph of the two of them I simply couldn't paint the man into the picture at all.'

He also died.

This clairvoyant quality in her painting is often seriously challenged in that many, who write to Charlotte Miller, give only the barest details about themselves: perhaps just their name and address. Yet looking through her letters at her home in St Ives, I frequently come across phrases like: 'You've hit the nail on the head!' 'I felt I must put pen to paper to tell you how accurate you were . . .'

'One day,' said Charlotte Miller, 'I was astonished to find myself painting something quite pornographic. Now as a conventional painter, I wouldn't dream of painting anything pornographic. Well, it so happened that the young woman who had commissioned the painting was a nymphomaniac and was right in the middle of a very sexy love tangle!'

Interestingly, though, the painter herself is not always 100 per cent accurate in her interpretations. 'In this picture there were three owls and several doors. I thought that they'd be starting a new life, but the couple ended up doing a moonlight flit.

Requests for psychic paintings, now come through the Crab Rock letterbox from all over the place — from as far afield as America and Australia.

'Generally I find the paintings very little trouble and most seem very successful with their messages. Some though concern me because of the sadness and I am unable to reveal the whole truth. And the letters that come back to me, from the people who've commissioned the paintings, often tell me my findings are extraordinary. Initially, I get quite a lot about the subject by just handling their letters, even before the painting is started. I have described their type of environment and what the subjects look like without a photograph . . . and various aspects of their life . . . I see these things so clearly . . . and I'm still puzzled by it all.

'However I mustn't give the impression that I only feel and paint sad, depressing things. Sometimes something very encouraging appears. There was the case recently of a woman, who wanted to be a writer, and I was able to indicate certain changes needed in her life style . . . and I'm hoping that this way she will really achieve her ambition.'

9
Dreams, Supernatural Smells
& Premonitions

The fascination of dreams is almost as old as Man himself.

Some primitive societies believed that the soul takes leave of the body during sleep and actually visits the scene of the dream.

Theories of dreams are many and various — some even curious.

Freud, the founder of psychoanalysis, believed that in our dreams we revert to thoughts of early childhood. He saw the need for disguising wishes which our conscious minds would not acknowledge.

I recall Dr Leslie Weatherhead, that brilliant Minister of the City Temple in London, once saying that if you dream constantly of stuffing things into a bag, and never quite getting them all in — or that you are running to catch a train but always just missing it — those dreams may indicate that, in the Yorkshire phrase, 'you've got too much on your plate.' 'I believe,' he said, 'that God speaks to us in our dreams, as much as He ever did, only we shall need a psychologist rather than a soothsayer to explain them.'

Many however would say that dreams are merely a simple form of expression which occur when the activity of the brain is depressed by sleep or under the influence of anaesthetics or drugs.

As someone, who dreams nearly every night of his life, I was surprised and disappointed to encounter only one dreamer in this whole Occult quest.

For some people, maybe only a small minority, dreams have a quality of premonition. One such person is Carole Eager, a housewife and mother of two children who lives at Whitchurch, Tavistock, Devon. 'It happened in June 1975,' she recalled. 'We had packed to go on holiday the following day — we were holidaying at a Pontins Camp at Wick Ferry — the children were excited, as were we, but I dropped off into a deep sleep within moments. I dreamed I was going up a flight of stairs, and I entered a very large room with a shiny floor. At one end was a raised-up platform and seated on the platform were a group of old women, each with a shawl over her head. I approached one and said ''Will you tell me my fortune?'' She shook her head, and pointed to another whose face I could not see. ''She will,'' she said. I approached the other woman. ''Will you tell me my fortune?'' She turned, and as she did so, I noticed that her face was an ashen skull. She pointed a bony finger at me: ''You will see Death!''

'I awoke in a cold sweat, and was so upset that I roused my husband and told him. He pooh-poohed the whole thing, and after a night of troubled sleep, I set off, with the rest of the family, the following morning.

'We arrived and settled in . . . we had not been there before so we spent the afternoon exploring. That evening we climbed the stairs to the great ballroom which shone like an ice rink and invited us to dance. At the end of the ballroom, the band played on a small rostrum . . .

'One of the Bluecoats — the children's ''Uncle'' was a middle-aged man, called Vic. He was a tower of strength and energy. In peak condition, he swam, ran, and played soccer as well as arranging games . . . the children loved him.

'I still had troubled sleep: graves and coffins and all manner of things, and my husband laughingly accused me of ''waiting for someone to drop dead''.

'On the last night, the Bluecoats put on a show. One item was a native dance, featuring ''Uncle Vic''. At the end of the number, the five dancers dropped to the floor to take their applause. Then they rose. At least four did. ''Uncle Vic'' stayed prostrate on the floor, and the others caught hold of his feet and amidst stamping and cheering dragged him off across the polished floor to the foot of the platform . . . But poor Vic never took the final bow. He was quite dead. He had died of a heart attack at the end of the dance, and my dream and the place of its happening were no more a dream, but a living nightmare.'

Apart from this prophetic dream, Carole Eager has something else which she calls 'my day dream . . . and although I never dreamed it and although it never happened to me, I'm sure it's a mental picture of an event that actually took place. I'm standing with a crowd of people on a narrow dark staircase that has a bend in it. We are pushed together like sardines and there is a door at the top of the stairs, and the crush of people goes on and through it. Yet we are not moving. Suddenly a man, in a flat cap, comes through the door; he pushes his way against the crowd and shouts "You're wasting your time. There is nothing for us!" He passes me and I decide to follow him back down. I push my way out using his back as my shield. We emerge into the light.

'Then there is a roar and dust flies everywhere. I look back and see that the staircase, on which I was standing, has collapsed into a mass of wood, dust and bodies. There are people screaming and a girl is hanging from a wall halfway up, showing long petticoats. I scream. The "dream" passes.'

★ ★ ★ ★ ★ ★

Another discovery in this quest for Occult experience was that Supernatural smells are rare.

One woman, whose nostrils have detected something beyond logical explanation is Nancy Stokes, a grey-haired, blue-eyed widow who lives in a cottage called Rosedene at St Pinnock Church Town, a few miles south of Liskeard.

Sitting in her sun lounge, one showery September morning, over coffee, Hampshire-born Mrs Stokes told me how she had answered a *Western Morning News* advertisement about six years ago. 'The result of that advertisement,' she explained, 'has been a complete mystery to me these last five years. Although I am a down-to-earth person I just cannot explain it away . . . it was all too real. This lady living near Lamorna, down in West Cornwall, wanted a companion-housekeeper for three months while her daughter was abroad.

'Anyway I applied and was given the post. I had not been there long when I had a sense of puffing and a smell, which I now know to be incense, although at the time I had never smelt it before . . . having been brought up all my life in low Church of England. I spoke to the lady of the house about it, but she wasn't conscious of it. I sensed it most when I was lying quietly in bed, although I also noticed it in the kitchen when I was sitting down quietly. The sense of puffing so distressed me that I had to force myself to stay there until the daughter came home. Otherwise I was very happy there. What was so strange was that the smell permeated my clothes in the wardrobe. At first, I thought it came from the wood, but it was the puffing under my very nose that so distressed me. I felt as if somebody or something was trying to get through to me. Another odd

88

30. Bodmin Moor: '. . . remoter parts of the Moor . . .
provide landscapes that must surely make the
cynics think again.'

31.   Doreen Spence, hypnotherapist of Paignton: 'I allow
myself to feel what my patient is feeling. If my
patient is crying, I will cry with him.'

32.   'When he came out of hypnosis, he said, "I can't believe it. I feel like a heavy load has been lifted off my shoulders." '

33.   Penwith coastline: 'Cornwall — or parts of her — have a
haunted or haunting quality.'

34. Berry Pomeroy Castle: '. . . I was very conscious of
atmosphere, something quite horrible in fact,
a real feeling of evil.'

35. Author Judy Chard: 'I've never seen a ghost, but I
believe in them. I haven't seen how television
works, but it's there . . . you just turn the
switch and you get the picture.'

36.   Holne Bridge: 'Some people say the Devil presides over
Dartmoor. Well, I feel absolutely at home there . . .
a benign spirit hangs over the place.'

37. Dartmeet: 'Devon and especially Dartmoor have triggered my writing,' says Judy Chard.

thing was that when I got back to St Pinnock, almost the other end of Cornwall, the smell still clung to some of my clothes . . . and only when they had been to the laundry did it disappear.

'Some months afterwards I was back in West Cornwall, having taken a holiday flat, with friends, at Mousehole. On the Sunday they wanted to go to the church, and we decided to go to St Mary's at Penzance — this was my first experience of a High Church occasion — and no sooner had the service started than the servers came out and started puffing out incense. Until that moment I had never smelt incense, at least so I thought, but immediately I recognised it as the smell I had smelt near Lamorna earlier. There was no doubt, at all, it had been incense. I then remembered that they had told me that the house had been by an old burial ground; so I feel sure I had been getting something from long ago. I never *saw* anything unusual in the house, but the daily help told me there was supposed to have been a ghost connected with the house.

'For six years I have wondered if there is an explanation to all this.'

One thing leads to another — they say — I was reminded of the fact as I drove into Bideford one showery November morning.

Bideford is to North Devon what Plymouth is to the South. Tennyson set the town in his narrative of *The Revenge* — a good choice for Bideford sailors manned many of the ships of the Elizabethan adventurers, serving under great Westcountry seadogs like Drake, Hawkins, Frobisher and Grenville. Five ships sailed out of this Torridge estuary to fight the Armada.

It is Charles Kingsley's choice too in that he wrote the greater part of *Westward Ho!* in a house that is now the Royal Hotel. You will still find him here, down by the river in marble, a pen and book in his hand.

My destination was Trelee, Park Lane, a quiet terrace away from the noise and the bustle of Saturday shopping and traffic.

It had all begun with two people and an AA box in Cornwall. The two people were Edith Watts, who some years ago lived at Lanlivery in South East Cornwall, and a friend Ethelwynne Brown, a former Mayor of Bideford who lived in the North Devon town and only came to Cornwall occasionally on council business. Mrs Watts, travelling

on a coach to Falmouth, one day, was surprised to see her North
Devon friend standing by the AA box just below Probus. It was a
strange story in that Mrs Brown admitted to being in Cornwall that
day, but she never used the phone box. Travelling on that same road
on the same date, though, she said she felt a tremendous urge to
telephone a relation in the county, but the commitments of the driver
of the car prevented her from asking him to stop. The story was even
more curious in that Edith Watts was able to describe, in detail, the
clothes Mrs Brown was wearing on the day in question. I have
recounted that strange Supernatural sighting in my earlier
Supernatural in Cornwall.

But Mrs Brown, hearing that I was writing a second book on the
Occult, had contacted me again about some additional experiences.
'I was out selling Alexandra Day roses one bright June afternoon
when I noticed that one of the terraced houses here which had been
empty for months now appeared to be occupied,' she said. 'As I
knocked on the front door, the next-door neighbour called from her
window: ''There's no-one there. The lady who came alone to live
there two days ago was taken to hospital this morning.'' I expressed
regret and asked her name and about her illness, but the neighbour
said she knew next to nothing about her, having not yet spoken to
her. The ambulance men had apparently only said, ''She's going into
hospital for observation.'' I continued on my way for a few minutes
thinking how lonely and sad the newcomer must feel and decided to
phone the then Vicar of Northam and ask him to call and see her in
hospital. I'll phone him this evening on my way home, I decided, but
I hadn't gone far before something insisted in my mind: No, do it
now!

'This meant interrupting my programme for the afternoon and
walking some distance out of my way for the nearest phone box.
The Vicar answered ''Thank you very much for telling me . . . I
shall be making my usual visit tomorrow afternoon and will certainly
see her.'' When I asked if he could go immediately, he replied
''Only with difficulty . . . and you did say she had gone in for observation only . . . so it's not urgent.'' Hearing my anxious insistence,
however, he said, ''Then, of course, I'll go now . . .'' Some two hours
later he came to see me, saying ''Oh, how glad I am you insisted on
my going immediately . . . I was just in time to say the Lord's Prayer
and hold her hand as she died.'' Not only was the Vicar able to
provide this comfort, but he was also the means of contacting the
98

family with the sad news.

'Then I had another similar sort of experience with a woman friend who in her late sixties became very depressed and had to go into a nursing home. I corresponded with her for some time and then heard from distant relatives that she had become much worse mentally, that she had been removed to a home in another town. The relatives died and I heard no more of my friend for some years and thought, no doubt, she had herself died meanwhile. Walking along the quay at Bideford one morning a sudden insistent thought came to me, ''Send a cheerful postcard to May. How ridiculous it seemed when I presumed her to be dead! But almost as though being impelled, I bought a charming flowered postcard at a nearby stationers and posted it to the last address my friend had been at. I had no answer. Indeed, I expected none, and soon forgot the incident.

'Nearly a year later I was lunching in a Plymouth restaurant when I heard someone exclaim ''How lovely to see you, Mrs Brown.'' I turned and there was my friend looking older, of course, but happier than I had ever seen her. ''Thank you very much for that lovely card,'' she said. ''I can no longer see well enough to write properly, but I was hoping I should see you again one day to tell you what it did for me. That very morning I had decided to do away with myself, and was actually on my way to doing it when your card arrived. It was beautiful and you finished your message with the words ''With my love as always,'' and because I felt somebody cared, I'm here today.'' She died peacefully in her sleep about five years later.'

'How do you account for these premonitions, these compulsive messages?' I asked Ethelwynne Brown as we talked after the excellent lunch she had cooked. Still a Bideford Town Councillor and now serving on the bigger Torridge District Council, it was hard to believe she had passed her seventy-third birthday.

'I wonder if some of us have a greater sensitivity to other people's suffering,' she said. 'I never knew my mother in good health, and later in life I cared for both my father and husband during long periods of illnesses. Perhaps that kind of background makes one more responsive, more sympathetic.'

'Perhaps, then,' I suggested, 'you should have been a healer.' Ethelwynne Brown looked thoughtful for a few moments: 'I'm not so sure about that. But it's interesting that you should say that because I remember my mother once saying that the touch of my hands on her did her more good than all the medicines she tried.

The strange thing is 'I'm not in the least bit Supernatural. Admittedly, I go to church, and religion plays quite a part in my life . . . but I'm not at all the psychic type. I have always been a sportswoman and as a girl at Truro High School, I played cricket and netball and even some Rugby! And, with my council work, I've often found myself the only woman on a committee . . . so you can see I really am quite a down-to-earth sort.

'As I see it, I've been merely the instrument of a kind of telepathy and in the light of these experiences I would now never ignore any insistence inside me. I'd always fear I was denying somebody something.'

Ethelwynne Brown, whose ancestry includes an interesting mixture of Cornish, Spanish and Anglo-Saxon, is quite convinced she has seen two ghosts.

'I came into the dining room,' she explained, and found the whole place bathed in a golden light, though outside like today it was a dull, grey day. There was a certain feeling of warmth in the room, and I was quite astonished to see my husband, who had died some time ago, sitting there in his chair. He was a misty shape but sitting exactly as George sat in that chair. I suddenly felt tremendously happy, and found myself going instinctively towards him to touch . . . but he gently vanished.

'The other occasion was upstairs, one evening. When my mother died, I felt rather bitter. As a small child, I remember praying "Please God make my mummy better . . . make her like other mummies." And that bitterness enveloped me when she finally died after a long, very long illness. I felt she had missed so much in life. I was standing in one of the bedrooms when her figure came through the wall . . . no I wasn't dreaming . . . I hadn't even gone to bed. It was early on in the evening, and I wasn't thinking of her at all. She came quite quickly across the room and disappeared from sight through another wall, and I got the distinct impression that she wasn't in the least interested in me. She looked very busy and very happy . . . two things she hadn't been able to be in this life. All bitterness went from me. I never grieved for her again, and my belief in a life after death was suddenly strengthened.'

10
Hypnosis

Doreen Spence at Paignton

Hypnosis may not be quite as old as the hills, but its roots lie deep back in history. More than three thousand years ago the Egyptians used hypnotic incantations to cure their sick. The ancient Greeks, the Incas of Peru and our own Druids all treated illness by inducing hypnotic sleep.

Paracelsus, that great Renaissance medical character, is reputed to have been the first to discover that patients respond to strong suggestion. The true father of Western hypnotism though was Franz Anton Mesmer who was born in 1733 and whose name still lives on in the Dictionary with the word 'mesmerism'. Following Paracelsus's methods, Mesmer found that he could cure people by talking to them while simultaneously passing magnets over their bodies. Orthodox doctors, fearing the loss of their livelihoods, hounded him out of his home town of Vienna. He emigrated to fashionable Paris and set up in practice there. Alas it was not the end of the fleeing, for he later left France for Switzerland — for the same hostile reason.

It was on a cold grey January morning that I left North Cornwall for Torbay. Snow was falling on Bodmin Moor, but less than two hours later Torbay was bathed in brittle spring-like sunshine.

Torquay has a hint of the Riviera — an impression intensified by the palm trees on the sea front. I suddenly remembered Napoleon here on his way to exile remarking 'What a beautiful country, how much it resembles the capital, Port Ferrajo, in Elba.'

Doreen Spence, hypnotherapist and psychotherapist, lives at 36 Dolphin Crescent, Paignton. One of the highest houses in all Paignton, it has a spectacular bird's eye view of the vast, graceful sweep of Torbay.

Some people surround hypnosis with an aura of magic. Doreen Spence, however, is not one of them.

At the very outset of our conversation, she made it clear that she did not see hypnosis as part of something under an Occult umbrella. 'I can't see how it can,' she said. 'We do though do automatic writing, and this might come under clairvoyancy. The subject is put under hypnosis, his hand resting on the table and a pencil in it. People might ask questions and he writes down answers automatically with his right hand. I don't take part in these activities; personally I'm strictly for the scientific approach to hypnotism.'

Despite that scientific approach, both Brenda Duxbury, my Bossiney Books colleague, and I felt we were in the presence of someone with a rare power, remarkable insight — and healing quality.

We met for lunch at the New Grand Hotel, Torquay, where her husband runs the hairstylists' salon. He told us that in their days in the United States he did the hair of Miss Universe contestants. Doreen Spence, herself, was once in the hairdressing business.

She has one of the loveliest voices I have ever had the luck to hear, soothing and immediately relaxing. I could listen to her for hours. Her green, blue eyes have a penetrating quality, the kind of eyes you meet only occasionally — you would remember them in a crowd and it's a shock to discover that for years she battled with blindness. 'When I couldn't see I worked by feeling as a hairdresser, and I made bead necklaces.'

After lunch, we travelled to her home in Paignton, and continued the conversation in her consulting room. Though I was presenting myself as a patient, and to be honest I viewed the prospect of hypnosis with some apprehension, I found myself becoming more at ease, more relaxed.

Framed certificates were on the wall. 'I'm a member of the American Institute of Hypnosis,' she explained. 'I did this after a course in psychology. I'm a member of the National Council of Psychotherapists, and took part in the European research group on sexual behaviour.'

Doreen Spence was born in Plymouth. 'My mother was from Woolwich, daddy from Plymouth so I regard myself as Devonian.'

'Did you inherit this ability to hypnotise?' I asked.

She looked thoughtful and then chose her words carefully. 'It comes to me that I think my grandfather did some kind of healing. But I feel this is my own thing. It all started in the WAAF. I spent two years as a balloon operator and another two years as a flight mechanic. When I was on the balloon sites they brought vans around with cups of tea and books, and I always chose books on hypnotism and psychology; they whetted my appetite. This was in 1941-42. I had done hairdressing before that. I read these books in the WAAF. I couldn't get enough of them, and I practised on the girls in the billet. Then I decided after the Air Force to go into it further and I went to the School of Psychology and Hypnotism in London. Then I went to America and there I studied from the beginning. I started professionally practising in 1964. In the State where I worked you had to be licensed and I had to go to the State County Court House and present my credentials.

I asked her how she defined hypnosis.

'As I see it at the moment, I see it as a heightened state of suggestibility.' She disagreed with a dictionary definition I had recently encountered: 'Hypnosis: the artificial production of state resembling sleep.' 'The artificial bit's wrong. You're not asleep at all, but wide awake. The brain wave patterns . . . they're all the same as in the waking state. They may *look* as though they're asleep, but there is some physical difference.

'There are various induction techniques. What I would use for one I couldn't use for someone else. I would use a more domestic approach for an old lady rather than a scientific one. I might only use a relaxation technique. I play it as it goes along. There are a variety of techniques according to the patient. You can't knock everyone out for six like a clockwork machine.

'Sometimes I use the Chevril pendulum — this is a clear ball on a gilt coloured chain. This is for focussing — you are upside down in it. If you take a piece of plain white paper and draw a 6 inch vertical line on it. Then tie the chain to a pencil and hold it like a fishing rod, in alignment with the vertical line, the ball will start to go up and down that line, and after a little while it will start to go into a circle, to rotate clockwise or anticlockwise according to your thoughts.'

Like the good spiritual healers I have met, Doreen Spence, though believing she is very different from that field, is equally modest about her personal contribution.

'If I haven't any gift, I won't spoil it for people who think I have. I don't cure anybody. They do it themselves. They utilise their own mechanism in the wrong direction. They don't see themselves in the right direction. You need to be taught the correct thinking vocabulary. They have given themselves an instruction of *can't* so the brain obeys that instruction.'

She is cautious about using the word 'cure'.

'If a cure happens . . . fair enough. There is about a sixty to eighty per cent success rate.'

'Why do the twenty or forty per cent fail?'

Now it was her turn to pose a question: 'Is it in their make-up? It could be that they need a few more sessions to get the hang of what I'm putting over.'

'Some people are more responsive than others,' I suggested. 'The word is *suggestible,*' she said. She has the wonderful knack of correcting you without the semblance of a schoolmistress. 'Most of the people have got the thing sorted out before they come, and most of them are recommendations. They know that they are going to be happy to put themselves into my hands. If they're anti me, it's wasting money. I have had a couple who didn't want to come. One man poured out his problems and I told him that from now on things would be different. When he came out of the hypnosis he said, ''I can't believe it. I feel like a heavy load has been lifted off my shoulders. And I didn't want to come in.''

'I once had a woman to see me who hadn't slept for fourteen years. She had tried psychiatrists, hospitals, drugs, pills. None of these had done any good, so she came to see me. I had to uncover things, and gradually she developed into a good hypnotic subject. Was it a sexual avoidance syndrome? I told her that post hypnotically she would be able to tell me with a flash of inspiration that would come in to her mind of something that had happened fourteen or sixteen years ago when it started. We tried it for two weeks. Nothing happened. She was able to tell me on the third week. She was pregnant and the baby was going to abort. At the time of the abortion, the doctor picked up the foetus in a tissue and took it over to the fireplace and put it on the fire. The woman was so horrified to see the baby going up in flames that it sent her round the bend. Her subconscious reaction to that was that if she avoided sex from now on she couldn't get pregnant and it couldn't happen again. Remembering the event released her from the insomnia.'

We then talked about the attitude of the medical profession. 'They're more co-operative now. They send patients to me from many parts of England. In fact, I went on a half-hour television programme with a panel of doctors who agreed there is a place for hypnotherapists working in conjunction with doctors. But Dr Zummerman of the British Medical and Dental Society . . . he said no one should use hypnotism . . . only doctors. But the doctors haven't had any training in hypnotism. Not in medical school. They have to take training courses from people like my colleagues and I. A patient told me he had been to another hypnotist, a *doctor*, to give up smoking. ''The doctor offered me a sniff of trialine gas, and the doctor himself had a sniff. After several sniffs, the doctor asked 'How do you feel?' I then asked him whether this was hypnotism. 'I'm not going to get anywhere with this lark,' I thought. So I asked the doctor 'Is this all there is to it?' He said 'This is it!' I then said 'I don't think this is what I want. Do you mind if I go!' 'No, I don't mind if you go,' said the doctor.'' So the patient got up and walked out!'

People can be very demanding, especially those with problems. 'How do you manage to keep on top form every day?'

'I think I switch my mind and allocate it to the patient and then when the patient's time is finished, I will then give myself half an hour to unwind. And sometimes if the session is dramatic then you really allocate all your mind at the time and then you switch on to become the little wife again afterwards.

'It's a conscious effort. I allow myself to feel what my patient is feeling. If my patient is crying, I will cry with him. The whole thing is acting itself out there in front of us and I am sharing it with them. I try to give them strength to get themselves together again and I put my whole heart into it.

'I need more time with some people. Uncomplex things like smoking and slimming are everyday things to get your teeth into quicker. Nervous problems, psychological things, take longer. Mass sessions are a little less compassionate and I don't waste unnecessary time then. There is no idle conversation. It's more businesslike. But when there is a one to one ratio, more conversation comes into it.

'I do quite a lot of mass hypnosis for charity, collecting money for hospitals, medical centres, etc.'

'The big sleep hits town every Monday at 7.30 in the medical centre at Torbay Hospital,' wrote a reporter of the *Torbay Times* in February 1977. 'Mrs Doreen Spence's hypnotherapy sessions, where she hypnotises people into giving up smoking, have attracted more than a thousand smokers in the last three weeks making this probably the largest mass hypnosis project in the world ever undertaken.

'The only sound in the room is her voice as the session begins. Some people are very susceptible to hypnotism and go into a state of complete relaxation at the second she starts to speak.

'Others need more persuasion. She moves quietly around the room, touching their hands and lifting the heads of those who have bent double in their chairs. About one hundred people hang on her every word and after a few minutes the atmosphere is so calm that the air conditioning seems to be roaring from the corner of the room . . .'

However my consultation with Doreen Spence had nothing to do with smoking. My problem was a curious mixture of claustrophobia and vertigo. I cannot use the London underground or lifts. But my biggest problem was an inability to use the Tamar Bridge; though I can venture on to the Cornish cliffs and look down a sheer cliff face an illogical something has stopped me from using that Devon-Cornwall bridge for more than ten years. On journey after journey to Plymouth, I have had to travel via Tavistock: a longer trip which, over the years, has cost me heavily in time and extra petrol.

Claustrophobia too has plagued me in theatres to the extent that I have been compelled to book gangway seats — or simply not to go. Yet illogically I can go to London and speak at an animal welfare conference to six hundred people without too much anxiety.

My hopes were now on hypnosis doing what will power had failed to do. I told Doreen Spence all this, and especially of my need to drive across the Tamar Bridge and yet the huge fear it irrationally generated inside me.

'If hypnosis is nothing more than suggestionism — self suggestion — make sure then you don't say "I'm petrified!" Your mind and brain will obey your instruction. Don't ever repeat those words you've just said to me,' Doreen Spence told me. 'Could you now try to use phrases like "I used to be afraid in the past, now I shall gradually be able to drive over that bridge without batting an eyelid." It's self-orientation. The mechanism isn't functioning when other people drive you — only when you're driving yourself. Perhaps as a child, someone pretended to push you over a high place.

'A lot of us have claustrophobic and vertigo tendencies. They might be put there for a reason . . . there might have been something wrong with our ears . . . we never know if the phobia isn't there for a special reason. Take it away and it might be replaced with something equally disturbing, or worse. You can get rid of one problem but still find yourself left with a question.

'Take allergies: some of them are deliberate ones the body cooks up against micro-organisms that the body doesn't want to have internally. I think a lot of these allergies are really protection for something else. A while ago surgeons were ripping out tonsils. Now they realise tonsils are there as blotting paper for micro-organisms. We shouldn't try to rid ourselves of allergic reactions, for something worse could happen. This *could* apply to your claustrophobia — it might be a safeguard — perhaps your ears. The brushes may be out of alignment, and it may be an inbuilt protection against this. It's perhaps a guideline to investigate oneself *within.* Some people can go up on the roof tops; others can't. Generally I don't think we should mess about with our patterning. But if the phobia makes the patient's life distressing, then I would be all for trying to do something about it . . . and the best thing may be to learn to relax . . . personally, I'm always learning.'

As I closed my eyes and leant back to begin this session of hypnotherapy, a strange fear came over me: dry lips and an embarrassingly loud gurgling of the stomach. I had read about fear of the unknown; now I was experiencing it. But it was fleeting. Suddenly that lovely, reassuring voice took away all anxiety. In a matter of seconds I had come from a bad nightmare into beautiful sleep — though sleep, perhaps, isn't the right word because all the time I was conscious of her voice. My hands were now at rest, my knees tired and my whole body felt heavy. A warm drowsiness covered me from head to foot.

My eyes were closed and I had no desire to open them.

I find it hard to say whether I was completely hypnotised or somehow transported into some delightful state of relaxation. But when I did reopen my eyes and return to conversation, I felt a different, better person.

Happily too that was not the end of the story. Ten days later, appropriately on my birthday with my wife Sonia sitting alongside me, I drove over the Tamar Bridge not once but twice in the same day. Initial apprehension, but ultimately tremendous satisfaction in knowing that an old enemy was losing its grip. And two Sundays later, in a party of four, I attended a packed concert at Truro to hear our great Cornish singer Benjamin Luxon. To the astonishment of the others, I sat three places from the end seat. I could not remember the last time I had done such a thing.

I wrote to Doreen Spence to tell her and thank her. It was a difficult letter as I simply could not find adequate words.

11
A Writer's Response

Judy Chard at Newton Abbot

The Westcountry has drawn writers like a magnet.

Some, already established authors, have come — maybe a form of hero-worship — following in famous literary footsteps, in the wake of D. H. Lawrence, Compton Mackenzie, Virginia Woolf and others. Some have come and suddenly — or slowly — found the urge to create growing inside them. ''The bones of this land are not speechless,'' wrote the perceptive Frances Bellerby. One woman agreeing with that sentiment is Judy Chard who, with her husband Maurice, lives at Morley, an old farmhouse a few miles outside Newton Abbot.

'Devon, and especially Dartmoor, have triggered my writing,' she explained. 'I have a great affinity with my dear old typewriter, but I sometimes wonder if I took it back to Kent or went to live in some large city whether the desire to write would be so strong. Devon's my spiritual home. Suddenly, one day, I discovered, quite by accident, that my grandmother came from Ide near Exeter. The news made me numb for several days, made me realize why I had immediately felt at home in Devon. Some people say the Devil presides over Dartmoor. Well, I feel absolutely at home there . . . a benign spirit hangs over the place . . . or maybe I'm one of the Devil's disciples and feel at ease there!'

A Scot with blue eyes, she is the easiest person in the world to interview. The words flow naturally, as naturally one guesses as she hammers them out on her 'dear old typewriter'. A novelist, short story writer, regular contributor to *Devon Life*, and a tutor in creative writing for the WEA in Devon, she clearly loves words and the wonders they weave. Her enthusiasm for them is infectious. We talked for more than two hours, and the hands of the clock seemed to accelerate astonishingly. I was reminded of Sir Neville Cardus' remark that 'all good conversation — and writing — is discursive.'

Interviewing her is a fascinating experience because, now and then, you realize that you too are being interviewed: the journalist and the broadcaster inside Judy Chard keeps popping out — a genuine interest in people and animals and the things which make them tick.

Her interest in the Supernatural is deep and diverse. 'I've never seen a ghost,' she openly confessed, 'but I believe in them. I haven't seen how television works, but it's there . . . you just turn the switch and you get the picture.' She gestured quietly with her hands. 'Radio waves are here all around us, but we're not picking them up. I think it's the same with the Supernatural. Of course, I suppose most people don't like to admit that they believe in ghosts, but even the most sceptical have been known to acknowledge, at least, a feeling of atmosphere, either good or bad, or that aura of coldness when a ghost is reputed to appear.

'When I recently visited Berry Pomeroy Castle, I was very conscious of atmosphere, something quite horrible in fact, a real feeling of evil. I now find it difficult to deny that the stories about the castle cannot have some authenticity. As you may know Margaret and Eleanor de Pomeroy were caught up in an eternal triangle, both in love with the same man . . . the elder, Lady Eleanor, mistress of the castle, locked poor Margaret in a dungeon and literally starved her to death!

'A writer from one of the glossy teenage magazines — down to earth and sceptical I'm sure — spent a night in this particular dungeon, or the remains of it, and on being asked next morning if anything odd had occurred, had to admit, although he hadn't seen a ghost, he had been aware of a peculiar vibration all night, like a slight electric shock . . . and intense coldness. Later when a newspaper from Torquay sent a man to take pictures, the camera which had worked perfectly outside the dungeon, simply refused to function inside.

'When I was at Berry Pomeroy I met a Mr Wilsman, the father of Sheila Ellis who has written a booklet about the ghosts and legends of the castle. Mr Wilsman lives at a farm nearby and he told me there have been many weird happenings to visitors who claim to have seen a ghost on the ramparts. One girl described exactly what it looked like, although she and her parents were complete strangers to Devon, never even having heard of Berry Pomeroy. "In fact," Mr Wilsman said, "many very sensible people admit to having seen things."

'Even more curious is this fact that there seems to be no record of anyone actually living in the Tudor part of the house, which Cromwell may have destroyed, although there is a theory that it was struck by lightning and burnt down . . . a theory that would fit in well with the long history of violence and murder — even suicide — that the castle is steeped in. The two young Pomeroy knights, who held the castle after the rebellion in 1549 when the edict went out that all castles must be destroyed, rather than submit to this degredation, hid their gold and valuables, then blindfolded their horses and rode them over the cliff into the valley below, choosing death rather than defeat.

'When I was at the castle there were flocks of jackdaws building their nests in the ruins and they seemed to resent very much my intrusion . . . the souls of the long dead Pomeroys? Fanciful perhaps; maybe a writer's imagination . . . but I couldn't help thinking and wondering.'

Judy Chard admits that she adores Dartmoor. 'Some people talk about the terror and the menace of the moor. Well, personally, I've never felt it. In fact, though I'm a Celt and very sensitive to atmosphere, I don't overreact; for instance, a lot's said about Wistman's Wood being eerie . . . I don't find it frightening or even all that dramatic . . . but interestingly there's a road on Dartmoor that gives me a feeling of discomfort. I don't feel anything if I'm driving along it, but walking that's another matter. The goings on there are even stranger and more sinister than Berry Pomeroy. It's that stretch of road across Dartmoor between Postbridge and Two Bridges. This road started to get a bad reputation in the early 1920s round the area known as Archerton. Pony traps were overturned for no good reason, a cyclist felt his handlebars wrenched from his grasp and ran full tilt into a stone wall, horses shied and bolted, a doctor from Princetown was travelling on a motor cycle with two children in the sidecar. The engine literally detached itself from the machine. There was no other description possible. The result was a major accident.

'An Army Officer reported an enormous pair of hands, covered in long dark hairs, taking charge of his steering wheel, covering his own. In fact, so authentic seemed these reports that in 1921 *The Daily Mail* sent investigators to the spot. The Local Authority had the camber of the road altered, but soon after there was more evidence . . . this time from a woman and her husband who had parked their caravan in the area. During the night she was awakened by a noise outside; looking from the window she saw an enormous pair of hairy hands scratching at the glass above where her husband lay asleep. She made the sign of the cross, and the hands vanished.

'Yes, rather too many coincidences. And then as recently as 1960 a man driving a car from Plymouth to Chagford was found dead beneath his overturned car, but when experts examined the wreck and his body, no reason could be given for the cause of the crash.

'But it's not only motorists who seem to be affected. Walkers in the area have told of a feeling of panic, similar to the dreamlike sensation when one is rooted, paralised to one spot. Auto-suggestion? Imagination? I don't know what the explanation is. One theory advanced to me is that some kind of malignant influence, an emanation from disembodied matter, neither entirely human nor entirely spirit, a halfway product . . . pervades the area. Perhaps the result of some kind of violence which occurred there in the past, a materialisation of violent death for this was once a thickly populated area . . . there are traces of Bronze Age burial kists . . . yes, like your cromlechs down here in Cornwall . . . burial spots.'

We were talking in the cottage, overlooking the valley, beyond St Teath. Outside an October afternoon turned to early evening — as shadows stretched on the slopes westward. Rex, a gentle Welsh collie cross, lay quietly, half asleep, half awake. Judy Chard is, in fact, a great animal lover.

'When I lived in a city, if someone had asked me if I believed in wart charming I should have probably backed hurriedly away, convinced, at the least, that they had a touch of the sun. But three decades of life in Devon have cured me of that sacrilege. In fact, when I took my dog to the vet. with thirteen warts of varying sizes . . . on the dog, not the vet! . . . he shook his head and said, ''Nothing much I can do, try a wart charmer.'' He said it in a perfectly matter of fact voice, and so conditioned was I that I didn't turn a hair, but just made enquiries as to where the nearest one lived.

'If anybody's really sceptical on the subject of wart charming, I'd refer them to the late Vian Smith, a writer who, if anyone ever did, knew his Dartmoor. He told the story of Mr J. H. Brackenbury of *The Ring of Bells*, North Bovey, whose wife bought a horse called Double Brown for thirty-five guineas . . . nobody wanted her because she suffered from warts. It seemed nothing would shift them, and the poor animal even had trouble walking. Mrs Brackenbury tried all kinds of remedies, all of which were useless, so she called in a moorland superstition . . . a wart charmer . . . he didn't even see or touch the horse. He merely assured Mrs Brackenbury, through a third person, that within a week they would be gone . . . within ten days they were! Was it coincidence or something else? Anyway the horse was restored to perfect health and eventually won a point-to-point race.

'But to go back to my dog and his warts, I was told of a white witch living on Dartmoor, but was warned that wart charmers can be ticklish customers, some being very proud of their gift, others shy and reticent. I decided to take a chance. The gate was wired, an exuberant collie leapt up and down like a yo-yo — the witch's "familiar"? Anyway it seemed I smelt friendly, the door opened before I could knock. For certain this must be a witch — she was so traditional as to be almost ridiculous, nose and chin practically met, wisps of grey hair framed the gaunt face, and one glass eye of fixed intent did nothing to dispel the image. I told her I had heard that "someone in the village could charm warts . . ." I had been advised to make an indirect approach. She drew me inside. The light was dim as dusk was falling, a log fire crackled in the grate, a table in the window was covered by a chenille cloth, glass cabinets held silver cups, china, photos and an ostrich egg.

'She confirmed she did indeed charm warts, but she had many other gifts . . . she had "reached out" to Australia to cure a young man of thirty-four who was "mazed" in the head, and returned him to his mother in the village, sane and in his right mind . . . she drew me to the window and pointed to the wonderful sweep of isolated moor . . . at the end of the garden was a holly hedge, there were seven trees with a whitethorn at the end, a portion cut away so a person could stand under it, and here be cured of every sort of skin disease — her speciality, she added proudly.

'She left the room for a few moments, and came back with an old cocoa tin — for one awful moment I thought it might hold "bats' wings, eye of newt, and toe of frog . . ." She chuckled at my shudders. "Tis only dock root, m'dear."

'My instructions were that I was to go home and dig up a similar root, wash off the earth, chop it into a saucepan, boil it for ten minutes, then put three drops on each wart. The only snag with warts, she added, was that they could be seven day, eleven day or even seventeen day ones . . . I must be patient. I'm sorry to have to tell you this is not entirely a success story. I carried out her instructions to the letter . . . our paddock is full of docks . . . within a fortnight the warts had disappeared from my black dog, but the brown one, who had never had a wart in his life, had thirteen . . . the exact number the other one had had! The two dogs disliked each other, so one might have put the curse on the other! More probably though the virus was caught by the other dog.

'I suppose I should have taken the brown dog to the white witch . . . that would have been interesting . . . but the fact was life was complicated just then: my husband was ill . . . and the brown dog was very old. Actually soon after he died.

'Yes, this curing of animals by charming and healing is interesting because it does make a nonsense of the mind over matter theory. I don't think it's a matter of belief by the owner, it's some communion between the healer and the animal.

'The curing of the young man in Australia, that's interesting too . . . this reaching out, thousands of miles, proves that sheer physical distance doesn't matter.'

Our conversation now switched to a subject which some may say does not come under a Supernatural umbrella: water divining.

'It's a difficult thing to define,' admits Judy Chard, 'but that shouldn't bar it, should it?' The question came with a broad smile creasing her face. 'It could be a mixture of things, partly a gift, partly a technique or country craft and perhaps partly Supernatural. A farmer taught me to use a hazel twig.

'This ability to determine the sex of an unborn child or animal, to trace missing persons, and to divine water, has always been surrounded by a certain amount of suspicion and disbelief . . . but there are thousands of us spread about the world who are able to ''dowse'', and the art is of special interest here in the Westcountry, as it was brought here by the Germans in the fifteenth century for the purpose of discovering the lost tin mines of Cornwall.

'History doesn't relate who really first discovered that water too could be found in this way, but apparently it was described by Cicero who died as long ago as 43 BC, although the actual word ''dowse'' is said to be Cornish.

'Some while ago I read in the press that one of the TV weather ladies had forecast the sex of her baby before he was born (apart from the weather!) using the needle, thread and cork method. She had threaded the needle, stuck it in the cork and held it over her left wrist — the cork swung back and forth once, stopped, and repeated itself twice, indicating that she already had three girls. Then it swung round and round, indicating that her next child would be a boy . . . all this information was correct.

'Apparently the Greeks and Romans used 'Y' shaped sticks for general dowsing, but there are many forms of instruments used, from metal rods, whalebone, etc., to the most usual - pendulums made of wood, glass or metal. As I said, I myself used a forked hazel stick, which has no special merit, but it is easily available in the countryside, and is pliable under pressure.

'You hold the two ends of the fork in either hand, the straight end away from the body, and as you walk over the ground, if there is water below, it will immediately become apparent whether or not you have the ability, for the twig seems to develop a life of its own, and pulls down with an almost irresistible force, in fact I have had it actually pulled out of my hands.

'People who are sceptical often can't believe their eyes when they do see it happening, which is understandable as they think they are being tricked, for not everyone can do it, although often, as in my case, one has the gift without realising it till someone suggests you have a go. It does take practice and skill before you can become expert, but I'm afraid my own efforts are very amateurish, but there aren't any teachers of the art, although there is a British Society of Dowsers formed in 1933 which has members all over the world, although when I recently contacted them they told me there were none in this area. It would be interesting to know if this has changed and if there are professional water diviners in the Westcountry. Many of the Society's members have been of great assistance to agriculture for determining the best grains for certain soils and so on.

'Some people have brought the ability to a very high degree of skill by self training and trial and error. In fact I read of a man who could test for decay in his teeth, holding his forefinger first against his healthy tooth, and then against what he believed to be a decayed one, using a pendulum. It first revolved clockwise and then anti-clockwise to show there was indeed a filling needed! Personally I have a built in sixth sense which gives me this information directly I get anywhere near the dentist's surgery!

'Dowsers also have an acute sensibility to changes in the weather conditions and atmospheric pressure, which seems to emphasise the fact that there is a connection between meteorological changes and radioactive waves from the ground, and in my personal opinion it has

114

something to do with the amount of static electricity in one's body, for I repeatedly get slight electric shocks from the metal of my car, whilst other people are not affected.

'Another explanation is that the relaxing of certain muscles and the reflex action thereon, can be refined with practice, like the receiving of radio signals by a wireless set.

'Another is that it is simply a gift handed down in certain individuals from the time when primitive man used it regularly in his daily life, and with the coming of civilization and scientific methods, the natural gift was used so little that it's become absent altogether.

'There must be some explanation of the fact that so many old castles, farms and other buildings have wells of great depths . . . they were dug long before the days of geologists and their sophisticated instruments. In the past dowsers were very important men . . . where water was scarce a great deal depended on their gift or ability . . . they worked alongside well-diggers and often could judge the depth, source and flow of the water from the twig's movements.

'I wonder if it works with oil or North Sea gas!

'Interestingly, there are far fewer women than men able to divine water. I wonder what that indicates.'

Finally, on the subject, Judy Chard had a few words of warning: 'In the sixteenth century Martin Luther condemned all practising dowsers as using Black Magic! But there isn't record of one being burnt at the stake!'

Perhaps inevitably our conversation ended with the Church and organized religion. Judy Chard had recently done a series of *Pause for Thought* broadcasts for the BBC's *Morning SouWest* programme from Plymouth. 'Some of my friends were quite astonished that I should be asked.' That broad smile swept across her face again. 'Truth is I'm not a regular church woman. I'm a kind of outside bulwark of the Church.

'Yes, I too think the present day parsons can look a bit ludicrous trying to be "with it"! I'm quite convinced of a hereafter. Ghosts, in my mind, don't prove the existence of a hereafter, they're just a by-product of it. How life ends in one way, and goes on in another, I don't know. We must be reabsorbed in some form or another. Maybe it's this thing I have about Dartmoor, to do with Nature and the countryside. We're all part of some masterplan.

'I certainly don't subscribe to the American idea that you weigh the corpse to see if the soul is still there!'

Postscript

Most journeys have a clearly defined end. You *know* when you have reached your destination. But bringing this Occult journey across the Westcountry to a close, and writing the end of this book have been fiendishly difficult. Because as Life goes on, so many of these stories go on too. There is no convenient final full-stop.

Take, for instance, the Bush Inn at Morwenstow, the fire there, they thought, had finished off all those inexplicable happenings. But the fire wasn't the end of the story, strange things rumbled on. Or consider people, like Barney Camfield and Doreen Spence, their different healing work continues and patients still benefit. Each day, in their working life, is probably worth another chapter.

As I am convinced death is not the end of the road, but merely a door opening, so I found many of these interviews resembling a door in that they led on to others. More than once on this journey I was reminded of Lady Clara Vyvyan who wrote of the Cornish atmosphere: 'It never beckons you on with unfulfilled promise.' That, in both Devon and Cornwall, was my experience. Indeed, one of the best stories of all, I declined to write: the family had suffered too much and was continuing to suffer. Their story alas is not over as a sinister something seems to pursue them from place to place. However I hope one day their experiences will see the light of publication. Indeed I am indebted to all the people, who appear in this book, for their help. They have made the journey so worthwhile. I have only been a kind of messenger.

SUPERNATURAL IN CORNWALL
by Michael Williams

'. . . a book of fact, not fiction . . . covers not only apparitions and things that go bump in the night, but also witchcraft, clairvoyancy, spiritual healing, even wart charming . . .'

(Jenny Myerscough on BBC)

'Serious students of ghost-hunting will find a fund of locations.'

(Graham Danton on Westward TV)

ISBN 0 906456 16 9

24 photographs

DEVON MYSTERIES
By Judy Chard

Devon is not only a beautiful county, it's a mysterious place too — and if anybody had any doubts about that, Judy Chard demolishes them with her exploration into the strange and often the inexplicable. This book though is not just about *mysterious Devon,* it's essentially about *Devon mysteries.*

'. . . my appetite for unexplained happenings has been truly whetted by Newton Abbot author Judy Chard's latest offering.'

Mid Devon Advertiser

ISBN 0 906456 29 0

22 photographs

**KING ARTHUR COUNTRY in CORNWALL,
THE SEARCH for the REAL ARTHUR**

by Brenda Duxbury, Michael Williams and Colin Wilson.
Over 50 photographs and 3 maps.
An exciting exploration of the Arthurian sites in Cornwall and Scilly, including the related legends of Tristan and Iseult, with The Search for the Real Arthur by Colin Wilson.

'. . . provides a refreshing slant on an old story linking it with the present.'
Caroline Righton. The Packet Newspapers

MY CORNWALL

A personal vision of Cornwall by eleven writers living and working in the county: Daphne du Maurier, Ronald Duncan, James Turner, Angela du Maurier, Jack Clemo, Denys Val Baker, Colin Wilson, C.C. Vyvyan, Arthur Caddick, Michael Williams and Derek Tangye, with reproductions of paintings by Margo Maeckelberghe and photographs by Bryan Russell.

'An ambitious collection of chapters.'

The Times, London

CORNWALL & SCILLY PECULIAR

by David Mudd. 48 photographs.
David Mudd uses his perceptive eye and his pride of all things Cornish to write entertainingly, at times with humour, but always affectionately, of some of the people, events, values and beliefs that create the background to Cornwall's strange and compelling charm.

'. . . one of the most important Cornish titles produced by Bossiney . . .'
The Cornishman

DARTMOOR PRISON

by Rufus Endle. 35 photographs.
A vivid portrait of the famous prison on the moor stretching from 1808 — with rare photographs taken inside today.

'The bleak Devon cage's 170 year history . . . fascinatingly sketched by one of the Westcountry's best known journalists Rufus Endle . . . the man with the key to Dartmoor.'
Western Daily Press

MY DARTMOOR

by Clive Gunnell of Westward TV — television's most famous walker.

Map and 12 pages of photographs and drawings of Dartmoor wildlife by Robin Armstrong.

'The work is that of a merry man, and an observant, though kindly one.'
Western Morning News

CORNISH MYSTERIES

by Michael Williams. 42 photographs.

Cornish Mysteries is a kind of jig-saw puzzle in words and pictures . . . though you'll find pieces are still missing, and that adds to the fascination.

'. . . superstitions, dreams, murder, Lyonesse, the legendary visit of the boy Jesus to Cornwall, and much else. Splendid, and sometimes eerie, chapters.'
The Methodist Recorder

ALONG THE DART

by Judy Chard. 34 photographs and 2 maps.

Judy Chard takes us on a journey up the River Dart from historic Dartmouth and the sea to its beginning on Dartmoor. It is a journey lovingly told. Past and present, people and animals, boats and buildings, she recaptures them all.

'. . . full of facts, anecdotes, and legends about the river and its surrounding area and people . . .'
Roy Derwent, Express & Echo

MAKING POLDARK

by Robin Ellis. Over 60 photographs.

The inside story of the popular BBC TV series.

'. . . an interesting insight into the making of the TV series . . .'
Camborne Redruth Packet

'It is a "proper job", as they say, and a credit to all concerned.'
Archer in Cornwall Courier

FOLLOWING THE RIVER FOWEY

by Sarah Foot. 49 photographs.

Sarah Foot follows the Fowey from its beginnings on Bodmin Moor to where it meets the sea beyond Fowey and Polruan.

'She stitches into the simple tapestry of the river's story names and incidents and anecdotes, deftly and lovingly, every thread and every page touched with charm and an unashamed sense of delight.'
Western Morning News

ST JUST IN PENWITH

by Frank Ruhrmund. 46 photographs.

'As did the miners before him, Mr Ruhrmund has fashioned a tunnel through the history of the area and he has struck many a valuable vein. With its outstanding photographs and beautifully descriptive text it is a book to be treasured.'

James Mildren, Western Morning News

PENZANCE TO LAND'S END

by Michael Williams and John Chard. 40 photographs.

A journey in words and pictures — brilliant photography by John Chard — incorporating Newlyn, Mousehole, Lamorna and Porthcurno.

OTHER BOSSINEY TITLES INCLUDE

THE BARBICAN
by Elizabeth Gunnell

TOTNES
by Elizabeth Gunnell

ABOUT THE CITY — a Portrait of Truro
by David Mudd

CORNISH SEA LIGHTS
by David Mudd

ALONG THE LEMON
by Judy Chard

ALONG THE BUDE CANAL
by Joan Rendell

ABOUT WIDECOMBE
by Judy Chard

ABOUT MEVAGISSEY
by Brenda Duxbury

THE FALMOUTH PACKETS
by David Mudd

ALONG THE CAMEL
by Brenda Duxbury and Michael Williams

TO TAVISTOCK GOOSIE FAIR
by Clive Gunnell

We shall be pleased to send you our catalogue giving full details of our growing list of titles for Devon and Cornwall and forthcoming publications.

If you have difficulty in obtaining our titles, write direct to Bossiney Books, Land's End, St Teath, Bodmin, Cornwall. Books 95p and over add 50p for posting and packing, books under 95p add 35p, hardcovers add 75p.